Broken to Branded

Amanda,
For your success!
My best,
R. Chington

Broken to Branded

Surpass your fears, find your purpose, and TAKE CONTROL.

Kat L. Chrysostom

ISBN: 0692062726
ISBN 13: 9780692062722

TABLE OF CONTENTS

PROLOGUE

One afternoon in 2011, my life's greatest blessing became my worst nightmare. And my world changed forever.

It happened in Ocala, Florida, the horse capital of the world. I had come here to follow my lifelong dream of working with horses. I was on my 16th horse of the day, a four-year-old who I'd never ridden before, and was riding him back to the barn. We were walking up a dirt bridge—a small bank over a large drop for drainage—when the horse tripped.

It's like a photograph in my memory: He had on bright blue side reins. I'll never forget that because I was looking down and I can still see a perfect picture of him falling, and those blue side reins are in that picture. Some people say he spooked at a golf cart; I don't know what happened. But he tripped, and we tumbled off the bank and both fell. He ended up passing away months later. Because he kept falling after that; there was some speculation that something was wrong. They don't know if it started in that fall or perhaps it was pre-existing, but I was the first person to have him fall with me.

I was lucky it happened at a horse show. It was a large horse show, and I was blessed that a lady Grand Prix rider saw our fall and knew immediately that it was terrible. She got off her horse and noticed that my helmet had flipped back off my head, with the chin strap gently stretched across my neck and throat. It was giving me traction and holding my neck stable. She was brilliant—she never took off my helmet, nor did the EMTs. This stabilized the fracture for the long ambulance drive to Shands Hospital in Gainesville, some 30 miles away. Up until they put me in the MRI machine, the helmet remained in place. To this day, my neurosurgeon tells me that had that helmet not been there, I probably would have died. It was a saving grace.

When I got to the hospital, I remember them talking over me, and vividly remember one doctor was strongly suggesting surgery while another was not. The latter was younger and wanted something less invasive, and the other gentleman had been around a long time. Neurosurgeons are some of the most negative people I've ever met in my life. I think that's partially because they're realists and see things solely from a scientific perspective. Plus, they see some of the worst traumas and illnesses—it would be difficult for anyone to remain positive in that field or one similar. Anyhow, they were saying they thought that permanent paralysis could result if they did the surgery, but it was still possible without it.

I was temporarily paralyzed due to the inflammation of my spinal cord. But nobody could tell what the actual damage was (if any) at that time because the injury was so fresh. But thank God, I did have enough strength to lift my hand to motion "no surgery."

I had a triple fracture in my C2 vertebrae, which is also known as the hangman's fracture—the same fracture as Christopher Reeve, the star of *Superman*, suffered. Reeve was also a horseback rider who was injured in a horse-riding accident; his accident resulted in paralysis from the neck down, leaving him wheelchair bound for the rest of his life.

In addition to the fracture, I had an array of other injuries—broken ribs, bruised bones, and pneumothorax, a condition in which air gets outside of your lungs due to severe impact, creating pressure and sharp pains in your chest. I was on a ventilator, and they put me into halo traction—basically a halo-shaped device screwed onto your skull to keep your head and neck completely still while you heal. It somewhat resembles a medieval torture device with four screws totaling 32 pounds of pressure to protect the spine from the weight of the head. They didn't sedate or anesthetize me for placement of that halo; they just locally numbed the skin and began tightening the screws.

That was the moment that changed my life forever. I remember it like it was yesterday: At the very moment when they began screwing the halo into place, I faced and accepted death, because I truly didn't believe I was going to survive.

But once I adjusted to the halo and learned how to walk and balance with this contraption on, I remember thinking, "Well, I made it"—and that redefined my life.

In the days and weeks to come, I came to realize I had to think of another plan for my life—show jumping, my passion up to then, was no longer an option. But besides my love for horses, I'd always had an entrepreneurial streak and a drive to succeed. And soon I'd have the opportunity to put both to the test.

CHAPTER 1

OPPORTUNITY CAN BE ANYWHERE

My company, Benefab®, was born from my struggle to recover physically, spiritually, and professionally. We offer therapeutic wearable clothing for both horses and people, which reflects both my lifelong love of horses and my new awareness of the importance of health and physical well-being. Our products are now available at tack shops and medical supply stores nationwide, and we're anticipating even more growth.

But this wasn't my original vision for a company. Instead, it's the result of several unexpected twists in the months after my accident. From this, I learned an important lesson: **Don't get too attached to your plans. A better one may come along at any minute.**

The accident, of course, was the biggest twist. After it happened, I was in the hospital for about two weeks before I went home to my parents in South Carolina to begin the long recovery process. I was in and out of partial paralysis for the three months while in the halo traction. During the first few months after the accident, I was heavily sedated—drifting in and out of consciousness. I would wake up and be exhausted again in five minutes. It was so different for me. Before, I had been really fit from riding so much.

And meanwhile, a lot of things changed—my world had stopped. Medical bills were racking up and things were just happening. Life was moving on, and I thought, *where are my opportunities?*

Luckily, just days before the accident, I'd gotten a job offer in New Hampshire, and despite my setbacks, the offer still stood. So as soon as I got out of my halo, I moved to New Hampshire. When the halo was taken off, I was put into a hard neck collar, which I was expected to wear for approximately three months. I ended up wearing that hard brace for over a year.

In my new position, I was an "assistant trainer." But in reality, I was a farm manager, which was something I could do from the ground. I was living at the time with one of the owners of the farm, and she was helping me as my mobility issues continued to persist.

About three or four months into the job in New Hampshire, I was able to begin weaning myself off the hard brace, as my doctors had instructed. But within days, I began losing feeling completely on my right side. I'll never forget the day: It was very difficult to get out of bed that morning. I was wheeled into the hospital, and of course, they saw me in the brace and knew that I'd been in a halo because of the obvious Band-Aids covering the bright red scars left on my forehead from the screw holes. It was apparent to anyone with any medical knowledge that I'd broken my neck.

This was a Sunday afternoon, and they were telling everyone the MRI machine was closed. And of course, it was the typical, full waiting area of an emergency room. But when they saw me coming, they immediately took me back and sent me to Dartmouth Hitchcock Medical Center, where they rolled me into the MRI, and that's when I knew: *Holy cow. This is serious.*

The neurologist there told me that paralysis can set in post-injury depending on the swelling caused post-trauma, potentially damaging the spinal cord. Until that day, I had been surviving, but this was when my fight really began. It made me realize I had to find another path professionally and start on that new path. Being on the ground around horses wasn't what I wanted to do. It was being with and on a horse that had brought me happiness pre-accident—but the reality of the situation forced me to reconsider these aspirations. Going back to what had been my safe place for my entire life had become a terrifying proposition.

It was either give up or start a new direction, and I'm not somebody who gives up. So, a new direction was the only option.

The idea of starting a business felt natural to me. When I was in high school, I developed a desire for success. We were an upper-middle-class family and I had the privilege of going to an elite, private high school. We didn't have what some of the kids there had—I had friends who traveled the world and had access to private jets. It was eye-opening to me because I'd never seen anything like that, and that's what really put the taste in my mouth for success.

My father is a successful businessman himself. He's a dentist, who built a very large dental practice, one of the largest in South Carolina. He instilled an entrepreneurial streak in me at a young age and taught me that you could do anything you put your mind to.

I think this set a strong foundation for my future. For instance, he would buy me a pony for resale, and he'd have me keep track of all the expenses. When it was sold, I would pay him back for his purchase investment plus expenses and we'd split the rest, fifty-fifty. So, it was sort of a business. This was what instilled in me that love of business and the love of the deal. People ask me, "How do you define success?" To me it's that drive, it's the idea of closing a deal no matter what it is.

I also thought about going back to school after the accident. Throughout school, I'd completed a minor apprenticeship under a neonatologist, and I've been very passionate about babies and their medical care since that time. My other thought was to become a dentist and help my family with the practice. But both of those seemed a bit daunting because school just wasn't my thing. I did well in school, but I was always better being my own leader.

But the accident changed all my plans.

I was really struggling to come back, physically and emotionally. And at the same time, I was trying to get my business off the ground. I've always had an inner drive, a yearning for more, that thing that makes you get up in the morning—whatever it is. But for the first time in my life, I would rather have stayed in bed, just because of the physical constraints. Obviously, having physical ailments can hugely affect your emotions, and I really struggled.

During the year after my accident, I had this fear—I didn't know what it was, perhaps a fear of the unknown. All I can tell you is that it was an overwhelming fear. Because of it, nothing seemed okay. And I am not a person to wear my emotions on my sleeve, so I bottled up a lot of that. It was a dark time for me.

And while I thought I was getting better, I wasn't healing nearly as quickly as I hoped. I remember the first time I tried to ride again after the accident. It was several months after I had gotten out of the hospital, and I honestly didn't think I'd have any problem with it—I'd get onto the horse and everything would be just like before.

But it wasn't. The minute I mounted the horse, I knew it was too much. We hardly went anywhere—I had to get off almost immediately. I just wasn't ready.

Riding had been my safe haven and my comfort zone, and now I was scared to death of horses. I had relentless nightmares. I was told that this was post-traumatic stress disorder (PTSD) from the accident, but I personally believe that what you can't fight off consciously, your subconscious gives you to dream about. So, nighttime really became the enemy for me, even though I'd slept like a baby for as long as I could remember. Perhaps I was also affected by sleep deprivation. I think a lot of things were playing into my emotional state.

And then one night, I hit absolute rock bottom.

I was sleeping with the lights on, because of this fear. And I woke up and had to go to the bathroom—badly. But the idea of getting out of bed terrified me. The very thought of putting my feet on the floor was horrifying, even though I knew that wasn't what I was really scared of. It was everything else. The fear of the future. The fear of having no purpose now that my riding career was gone.

I was too overwhelmed by fear to even coax myself out of bed, yet I urgently needed to go to the bathroom. You can guess what happened next.

When I woke up in a wet bed the next morning, I swore to myself I wouldn't let that moment define me. I knew it was time to start looking past my fear and move on to the next stage of my life.

And that day, I got a sign that I was ready.

I'd been reading a lot of books, newspapers, and magazines during my recovery, and an article I happened to read around that time was about Shanghai, where there were more millionaires per square mile than anywhere in the world. And I thought, "Well, that's interesting!" So, I brought it up with a businessman involved at the farm, who had also become a good friend. And he asked, "Well, have you ever been to China?" When I said no, he said, "Would you want to go?" And the minute he said it, I said, "Well, yes, that would be really fun—let's go!" After all, what else was I doing?

That trip to China turned out to be the start of my brand, Benefab®.

Honestly, I went there on a whim. I was originally considering exporting horses from Europe into Beijing, because the horse industry over there was, and is still, growing. We were both intrigued by the idea, but once we got there, it was increasingly apparent for many reasons there was little to no opportunity for that.

Before the trip, the neurologist at Dartmouth Hitchcock had recommended far-infrared light therapy for my neck, which really helped me get back enough movement and flexibility to travel. It also made the scars on my head less sensitive and helped them heal more quickly. And while I didn't know it yet, it would also give me the idea for my company.

While we were in China, we went to HORFA—an equine trade show in Shanghai. I had never seen anything like that in my life. Shanghai was wild! I think what made it wild for me was all the energy. I grew up here in America, the greatest country on Earth, where there is so much opportunity, but people don't necessarily go after it. And what really set Shanghai apart for me was that the people there are go-getters—they're not walking places, they're running. Literally. And I think that energy and competitiveness are special.

On my way to HORFA, we accidentally went into a job fair, and that's when it really hit me—wow, people were truly *running* for opportunities. The rush of energy in that room in Shanghai was just incredible. It sets a whole other level of pace. And I just happened to stumble upon it on the way to the trade show.

People live for opportunity there, they want something better—they don't have what we have here. The energy here is a lot lower overall—I think it's special to see someone in America really running for opportunity. But there, people jump at any chance they can to make their lives better because the alternative is much worse. They want more, but I don't think half of them even know what "more" really looks, or for that matter, feels like. That drive makes you feel alive.

We live in one of the greatest countries on Earth, and because of that, people tend to become lazy and/or entitled. In other countries, they're seizing the opportunity, while we sit back and wonder if the risk outweighs the reward. **When the alternative of staying in the same place is worse than taking the risk of potentially bettering your situation, people make moves.**

Have you ever wondered why an overwhelming number of small gas stations you walk into are owned by immigrants? That's because starting in the 1980's, Middle Easterners got a foothold in that industry by buying convenience stores in areas disadvantaged by crime, location, or other reasons. They could buy the locations cheaply and with little competition because the larger chains and/or individual Americans didn't want to take the risk. According to New American Economy, 40.2 percent of the Fortune 500 firms in 2016 were founded by immigrants and/or their children. In 2014, 19 percent of Middle Eastern and North African immigrants in the US were entrepreneurs, 11 percent of foreign-born Hispanics were self-employed, and 10.6 percent of foreign-born Asian immigrants were entrepreneurs. That same year, only 9.5 percent of working Americans were entrepreneurs.

And I was determined to be one of them.

While we were at the HORFA trade show, we went our separate ways, looking at different things, exploring the aisles, and we somehow met back up at a booth full of ornate, beautifully colored leather saddles. As we turned the aisle away from that booth, this Taiwanese man a few booths down exclaimed in English, "Oh my God, Americans!" He was so excited to see two Americans.

He had fabrics that he had formulated that could supposedly do what red-light therapy does—this was the same therapy I had gone through after the recommendation from Dartmouth Hitchcock. My partner was a bit lost as he had never heard of the therapy, but I was captivated. I kept thinking, "Oh my goodness, I want to know everything about this; this can help me." And here was this man with this idea: He had a lot of very technical fabrics infused with minerals and he thought somehow, in some way, they could be used in the equine market. He had flown there from Taiwan, and we exchanged business cards. When I got on the plane to go home, I couldn't stop thinking about it—and I thought, *this is my opportunity*.

I believe that when you have an opportunity, if you don't take some step to seize it within the first 30 minutes, it's likely going to be lost. So immediately I thought, *okay, I'm going to write him an e-mail*, and when I logged into my inbox, he had already written me!

My next trip was to Taiwan, where I got to visit his factory. He had not finished perfecting his fabrics, so I was involved in the finalization process. And that was the start of it—the start of how I came to design a line of braces, blankets, and an array of other therapeutic wearables, all starting from his fabrics.

It was a crazy journey. You know what's funny about it, and it's one thing I always tell fellow entrepreneurs, you can become married to an idea, but you have to be open to change. The reason I went to China was to possibly export horses from Europe to China, but then I came back with a therapeutic fabric that I soon began building a product line around. That trip would have been a complete failure had I just looked at that one angle and said there was no opportunity to export horses. But instead it was a complete success. **This defines a concept that's very important to me: the idea of *failing forward*.**

I wish I could say I had this fantastic idea for a business right then and there, but to be honest, I didn't know exactly what I wanted to do with that therapeutic piece of cloth. But I knew the idea had legs and I should see where it would run.

CHAPTER 2

FIRST STEPS

When I came back from Shanghai, I can't begin to tell you how much I didn't know. I had the drive and ingredients, but I knew nothing about what it would take to build a business. And while I had some funds—I had saved up quite a bit of money, and I was working—I had no idea of the extent of funds that were going to be needed for a startup. I didn't go to school for this. I now like to joke that I have my MBWA—my Master's in Business by Walkin' Around.

At that time, having a focus and a goal was so helpful. I've found that having any end goal could keep me going. When I was coming back from my accident, I had a goal to simply walk on the treadmill for five minutes at a time. Sounds simple, but that was very hard. It was amazing how much of a toll the accident had taken on my body, and just accomplishing that small (big at the time) goal made me feel a lot better, by being able to focus on and reach something—even if it's a small five-minute or ten-minute goal, it's an accomplishment.

I've found that goals need to be attainable—both for personal life and in business. I see people set huge goals such as becoming a multi-millionaire, and if they don't achieve it within a year, which likely they won't unless they're starting with a million in the bank, they become defeated. This is setting yourself up for failure. It's okay to make a large big-picture goal, but I've found it's more effective to set smaller, attainable goals with deadlines under that big picture. Huge benefits come from just knowing what direction you're going. **I always remind myself that a goal without a deadline is just a dream.**

If you're crystal clear on what your goal is, you're a lot more likely to achieve it. And that's something one can implement easily. There's a study that was conducted years ago by Harvard students proving that you're 80 percent more likely to accomplish a goal if you've written it down. I write all my goals. If I really want something, I'm going to write it down, and I'm going to plaster it where I see it every day—preferably multiple times a day. I grew up seeing that done in our household, so I was blessed having that mentality etched in my brain at a very early age.

I think a lot of the darkness and negativity I'd been experiencing before re-flected my physical ailments, but it was also a reflection of not having a focus—a goal or direction.

Focusing on my goals helped me recover and move ahead with my new busi-ness. Both of these things gave me a new direction and confidence in fulfilling my future.

I was still working in New Hampshire when I started the business—I wasn't willing to totally give up that stream of income. And I wanted to know there was enough traction before going all-in.

I was still working full time managing the farm, and the hours were a bit scattered, which worked in my favor. On rainy days, the farm would be closed. I would go down early, work a few hours, and not be back until the evening. On busy or slow days, in every single moment of spare time, I was building this business.

Most of the time, I got into my office early, around 4AM, because I had to be down at the farm by 7AM. I would work steadily for those few hours and then stroll down to the farm. And on my weekends off, I would travel to walk through trade shows, meet and talk to other people who were in the industry, and learn as much as I could. I researched the industry for about three months, and I also had a very comprehensive market analysis completed of the whole equine mar-ket; I wanted to locate what the market stats were and its growth. After three months, I dove in and started.

When I started Benefab®, **the first things I tackled were the basics: figuring out what the company would be called, what we'd be mak-ing, and what the target market for our products would be.**

I had originally chosen the name Quest—I liked the name because it was generic, and I thought it was fitting. After all, the business was a quest to find a way to rise above the accident.

So, I started marketing, and I had that name for almost a year. And just when I started getting some traction, I got this piece of certified mail from a well-known, large pharmaceutical company that owned the name Quest. It was a cease-and-desist letter, basically saying I had to stop everything—stop sales, remove marketing literature from the marketplace, and take down the website.

And when I got that letter, I was devastated. I had built a website, I had branded everything with this name. I didn't know where to go from there. I called the attorney that sent the letter and I just said, "that's fine" because I was afraid I was going to be sued. I didn't know what was going to happen, and I knew I couldn't fight them. I did a quick Google search, and thought, "this is not up my alley!" I didn't even have an attorney at the time.

I think their lawyer was surprised—*was this person really going to stop without a fight?*—but I didn't dare go and fight. I was afraid they were going to shut down my business entirely.

I obviously had to stop selling. I prayed a lot and I cried a lot that night, and the first thing I did the next morning was start making phone calls. One of the first was to the lady who had developed my website and the people I'd worked with on the logo design.

And it was amazing how people came together. The web designer offered me an amazing discount to design a new website, and the logo designer started working with me, also. It took about a month and a half to come up with the name Benefab®, but Benefab® makes a lot more sense: It stands for beneficial fabrics—the mineral-infused fabrics I discovered in Shanghai were the heart of my products. I re-branded all my inventory, designed a new logo, launched the new website, and got going again.

On the upside, I did have enough traction for them to find me, so I must have been doing something right! But thank God it happened then and didn't happen even further down the road.

I would say this experience definitely triggered my fears of the unknown, because I didn't know how to get out of that mess or where I was going to go. Had I accepted this as defeat, my business wouldn't be today, nor would you be reading the words on this page.

But this was also a great example of putting one foot in front of the other and not being crippled by fear of the unknown. By reaching out to as many people as I could, I rebranded my business, and really, I did it much better than the first time because I knew the roads better the second time around. I'd done it before and knew a lot of mistakes to avoid. I also knew market prices for things, so I could better negotiate contracts. I knew our target customer, so the website design spoke to that demographic—I was able to do it all twice as well the second time around. And, of course, I retained an attorney who had researched the new name.

Getting to that name was a process in my own head. I knew I needed something that wasn't too gender-specific but had a feminine flare (to cater to much of our customer audience). I wanted a look that was bold and assertive—a design that encompassed our company personality. Those are just a few of the thoughts that went into the logo design process, but I didn't necessarily know any formal way of organizing these ideas.

In retrospect, I realize there's a lot that goes into choosing a brand name, such as making sure that the name can be secured and getting trademarks and URLs. But luckily, I learned that all you need to find this preliminary information are mostly free searches—you can use GoDaddy.com to see if a URL is available, trademarkia.com to search for trademarks and their availability, and Google.com/patents to search the United States Patent and Trademark Office (USPTO) database. Of course, you can do basic searching on your own, but I highly recommend retaining an attorney before making any major decisions.

An important early lesson for me was there are so many things available at your fingertips with technology, and you should use them to your advantage. Why waste the time and money applying for a name when you could have found it was already taken? (Yes, I should have known this when I started!) Or create something that was already patented? First and foremost, do your research and don't make the same mistake I did! I had to learn this the hard way.

Meanwhile, I was still managing the farm while all this was happening, and I was getting Benefab® off the ground. People would call our office number, which is still the same number we have today, but back then, calls were forwarded to my cell phone. One day, I was at a horse show, managing the horses there, going down the aisles of the barn, and my phone rings. I'm answering for Benefab®—"Hello, this is Kat"—and a kind lady was on the other line. She'd called to purchase a pair of socks, and she quietly asked, "Is that a horse in the background that I hear?" I had to laugh—if people only knew! It was funny. We'd done an advertisement in *Diabetic Living* promoting our socks as beneficial for neuropathy, and she was calling because of the advertisement, so she knew nothing about our relation to horses. I replied "Yes!" and her exact words were "Oh, interesting..." Perhaps slightly weirded out, she still bought the socks! The reason I'm telling you this story is because you just do what you must do when you're getting started.

Once the business started to gain some traction, I knew it was time to move. I left New Hampshire in 2013, late 2013, Thanksgiving, actually. I didn't know where I was going, but I had some product and I realized my lease was up, so I needed to make a decision. I stayed about a month and a half in South Carolina with my family during that time. I was looking at different places. Texas was on my radar because I thought it was a central location to ship from, but from an equine standpoint, I've always loved Ocala. Known as the "horse capital of the world," it was the place to be.

Originally, I came down and I stayed in my fifth wheel—an RV—which I lived in for four years before finally purchasing a house! I went all in, making ends meet and working as hard as I could. It wasn't a pop-up camper, mind you, it was nice and spacious (as spacious as a camper can be), and it served its purpose. I thought if I had to move the business or shift focus, I could do it quickly; I wasn't locked into a lease, I owned my asset, and it was on wheels.

I've always been very realistic about entrepreneurship and small business. Statistically speaking, you're extremely likely to fail. According to *Forbes*, an astonishing 80% of entrepreneurs who start their own business fail within the first 18 months. That's 8 out of 10! These failures are a result of many factors including but not limited to lack of funding, need, or uniqueness of offered products and services, customer relations, lack of communication and leadership, lack of a profitable business model and one last thing that you can never discount—luck.

Expert Tip: Failure Is an Option

Remember, luck is that elusive quality which hides in all the cracks and crevices of fate and makes its appearance (or not) in one's life on its own schedule.

I recall my nephew, Ryan, who had quit a very good job to begin a very shaky new venture as a competitor to his former employer. It did not go well. After going through several hundred-thousand dollars of his own money—and some from friends and relatives—he tried to make another trip to the well to refloat his sinking ship. Ryan attempted to rope me into the futile task by dangling dinner in front of me and making his pitch "al dente" at an Italian bistro. After the pasta and red wine, he received the bad news that his appeal had encountered a severe case of indigestion.

By dessert, I had informed him that I had absolutely no interest in assisting him in digging an even deeper hole than he was currently in. I also wondered what his plans were in the event he managed to reduce any new funding to a smoking pile of insolvency. He confidently told me that "failure is not an option." I confidently replied, "failure is the most likely outcome." He smiled—which was the last time he did that for quite a long time.

-Commercial Real Estate Investor

With eyes wide open, I went into this venture thinking "let me see if this is going to work," and in early 2014, I signed a lease for office and warehouse space, and I moved everything out of New Hampshire. For a very short period between Thanksgiving 2013 and Spring of 2014, I had a fulfillment center in New Hampshire shipping the product to customers. The fulfillment center nearly killed me with pricing and storage fees. It cut my margins tremendously, so I thought, "I've got to get out of there and make a decision!" and that's what really forced me to make that decision. The Ocala area has very reasonable rents, but I looked quite some time for the right space and found the one we're still in today. It was a little bigger than I needed at the time, but it was reasonable enough, and now we're thinking of taking over the unit next door because we're growing out of it. It's been a fun progression.

I lived in the RV for just under four years, and that was a really good time of my life, from a personal standpoint. I realized that one, I didn't need a whole lot of space as I was so focused on working really, really hard; and two, I felt safe. I felt like I hadn't totally overdone myself—I feel like a lot of entrepreneurs that I meet spend every dime they make. So, I think for me, it was a good time to be a little bit of a chipmunk, to put things away and try to decide where to go next. And for simplicity purposes, it was great because it taught me you really can do big things without a lot. Not necessarily monetarily, but materially. When I moved, I sold all my furniture and the only things I kept were close to my heart. When I bought my house, I had to start over, but that whole process taught me a lot, including how to live well on a small scale.

I'm living proof that you can fake it till you make it—or better put, that you can "fake it 'til you become it," as Amy Cuddy says in her very popular TED talk: *Your Body Language May Shape Who You Are*. If you haven't watched it, I highly recommend it. In the sales and marketing meetings I was doing during that time, nobody ever would have believed I lived in a fifth wheel with no washing machine! And I hardly believed I belonged at those meetings. (My place actually did have a washing machine, but you could only wash two pairs of jeans at a time. So, I went to a laundromat for four years.)

It also taught me to appreciate things. Going to the Marriott felt like a vacation. I wouldn't change that—if I could go back, I wouldn't change a thing. It was part of my ever-evolving journey, and that's really what it's all about. And as this journey continues, it's become more and more about relationships for me and the people I've met along the way. You know, if you're in it for the money, then perhaps entrepreneurship isn't the way to go—I'm not saying I'm not into the money aspect of it too, any entrepreneur is (if they say they aren't, I'm calling their bluff)—but from a personal standpoint, the journey is what really matters.

But still, at first, it was a stumbling process of learning and a steep learning curve at that. Now, looking back, I wonder "How did I ever survive the first two years?" I didn't know exactly where I was going in the beginning, but I knew it was somewhere, and I was running as fast I could to get there.

Our first product was a scarf because I wanted one for my neck. Its fabric was made from a bioceramic polyester thread. These same minerals are what we use to this day; they've been proven to improve blood circulation and reduce inflammation, since they emit the same wavelengths as the far-infrared light therapy used in my recovery. This had a lot of resonance for me because far infrared light therapy had given me back my life, and I thought it could do a lot of good for other people and their animals.

When the scarf arrived, it looked like you got a pizza cutter or scissors and just cut the cloth into a long rectangle. The edges weren't sewn, and it looked unfinished. It was just a piece of fleece with a tag sewn onto it.

Still, I was so proud of it: Gosh, it was my first finished product! There was no hangtag, there were no brochures to go with it, but it was a start.

If I'd known then what I know now, I would have thought, "Wow, we're missing a lot of pieces," for sure. The tags didn't match the fabric, the edges weren't finished, there was no packaging to speak of—there were a lot of things that needed to be done. But I didn't notice before, and I think it's important to know that it was a starting point. I always say, "good is good enough," and it's true—it doesn't have to be perfect. If the first version is finished, then you've created a good starting point. **Don't obsess over perfectionism.** That scarf was my starting point, and it was good enough.

Now our scarf has beautifully finished edges, matching tags, sewn labels, professionally designed hangtags, brochures with nice packaging, and they're manufactured with selected seasonal Pantone colors for the greatest appeal.

We went from using standard Paint software to Photoshop and Adobe Illustrator, and from designs I made myself to professional designs by graphic designers. We now have washing labels and all the correct things needed to pass through duties and customs for entrance into the US. As the business grew, we put these things into place, and new things will continue to surface and evolve as we continue to grow. Overall, our branding and designs have been enhanced as well as the packaging. It's almost not recognizable anymore, but the basic core value of our products remains the same. It's been an evolution, and with every order we get better and better. It's part of the growth process. The quality has always been there, but the pieces needed to come together for us to create more of a finished product. I don't think any small business comes out with a perfect product line to begin with.

My main plan at first was for our products to be more horse-oriented—blankets and braces for horses—because I wanted to find some way to stay in the equine industry. And I thought that there was an opportunity there. To be honest, at the time I thought the horse industry was far larger than I now realize it is. It's very much a niche market. This isn't necessarily a bad thing, since it allows us to be a big fish in a small pond. **Niche markets can also serve as an excellent sounding board and place to refine your idea before taking it to a greater audience.**

If you're not familiar with the equestrian scene, you might be wondering why horses would need therapeutic products like ours. Basically, horses are athletes. If you're an athlete, say a marathon runner, you take care of your knees, your back, and other joints—perhaps you do cold and hot therapies and utilize whatever products you can for relief and recovery. It's the same for performance horses. They're very well taken care of: They're cold-hosed when appropriate and get warm therapy when necessary. They need all the same things—their backs get sore, as do their knees, their hocks (hind knee joints), and many other areas. They also get stiff necks, so a lot of our products, such as mineral-infused blankets and therapeutic leg wraps, address these problems.

I knew horses inside and out, but on the business side, there was a lot I didn't know—like just how to organize my day and get things done.

Typically, customers were my priority, which is something we've never lost sight of and that has helped us tremendously. Even if something had to be done on the back end, I would drop everything to answer the phone for a customer. For instance, at the very beginning, I was answering probably two to three emails a day about the company. I was reaching out to different people, searching for help to make things easier, and trying different strategies for effective branding—I didn't have any employees whatsoever at that time. So, whenever I got an order, I would drop everything I was doing, run down to the warehouse and ship it—and that would take a chunk of my day. Not exactly the most efficient use of my time!

Learning to market my products was also a steep learning curve. I remember sitting at my trade show booths the first year twiddling my thumbs wondering what I was doing there.

My first trade show is still etched into my mind, and not in a good way. It was the Horse World Expo in Baltimore, Maryland. I was supposed to fly in, but I didn't have enough suitcases to fit my setup. I'm not normally a procrastinator, but I went to TJ Maxx the night before to buy a bigger suitcase—it was a giant Timberland suitcase, which mind you, I still have today as my trade show suitcase (there's always a debate about who will have to carry it because it's so heavy with the 4+ years of tradeshow-must-haves we've accumulated!).

When I got to Baltimore, I rented a car. At the time, I was underage for renting a car, which is a whole other story, so it was outrageously expensive. And I thought, "My gosh, this is a huge investment considering how everything is adding up!" So, I drove to the show venue in the little Prius that I had rented, and there were hundreds of big trucks that were offloading pallets of setups, and there I was there with my two suitcases and a Prius!

I'd been to events, like small fairs and markets, but I'd never been to a trade show of this size. I went in and I was totally intimidated.

I collected myself, checked in at the information desk, and started feeling excited about the opportunity as I looked around. It took me a long time to find my booth. I get to it, and it's this small ten-by-ten booth with one lonely table in the middle. Most of the people around me had elaborate setups, like wooden barns and entire stores—huge, extravagant setups. And here I am with this little folding chair and one table. I displayed everything I brought in the suitcase and I thought, "I've got to get some color in here!" So, that night, I went to Wal-Mart and bought a couple of plants. Again, it was a start!

The first day I was there, I had no orders. The second day, I was talking to some people, but I think I looked kind of pathetic and again, no orders. The third day, I talked to some people, and one of the ladies said she might come back. I remember this so well because it was the first sale I ever made at a trade show. She came back the last day, and she bought one saddle pad. I didn't have any inventory there, so I had to ship it to her (lessoned learned: If you are going to a trade show, have inventory to sell and the ability to take orders). It was a $60 saddle pad that hardly made a dent in my whole investment in that show, which cost me altogether about $3,000.

I think the vendors in the neighboring booths felt badly for me, so they ordered each of themselves some product. They were very kind. I still keep up with one of those ladies. Every time we speak to each other, she says "I'm so amazed at what you've built, good for you!" She was there for me at the very beginning. We laugh about that still today.

So overall, I ended up with about $500 in sales, which I admitted was terrible, but it was a start. And I knew what needed to change. I really didn't have the setup, nor did I know what I was going into. And I had no inventory (only samples). So, how do you sell?

I learned my lesson, and the next time I booked a big trade show, I walked the floor before going, and I came with my entire setup and was ready to go. To get into most trade shows, you apply before being accepted. So, I'd take that time between the application and acceptance to talk to other vendors and refine my setup. And I did a lot of networking at that first show—I met the lady who still today helps me with some marketing as an independent contractor. At each show, I make a lot of new contacts. At that first show, I met a few people who taught me a lot about the industry, and some still keep in touch. The trade shows are good for sales and branding, but they are also great for networking with people within your industry as well as recognizing trends and industry movement. Even if you can't attend a trade show as a vendor, just walking it can be very beneficial.

That first year was a huge learning experience for me—and I'm still using the lessons I learned then today.

CHAPTER 3

SO WHO ARE YOU, ANYWAY? BUILDING A BRAND IDENTITY

Know Your Market

Once I started Benefab®, I soon realized that even though I'd grown up in the equestrian world, I didn't know nearly as much about it as I thought. I grew up in the hunter-jumper discipline primarily. I was in the hunter and jumper worlds, which are separate from the dressage world and totally separate from the rodeo world. There are many different sectors of the equine market and becoming familiar with them was a learning process. **Until you sell products and get feedback, you are not the expert you think you are.**

That really caught me by surprise. I know this industry inside and out, but I didn't know the marketing aspects of the industry. Being on the back end was very different from riding a horse and going into a tack shop as a consumer. And you really can't appreciate that until you're on the other side.

What made it tough was the industry is a bit old-fashioned, and it's very insular. I think for the most part, people in the horse business are hard-working people who are out from dawn to dusk and don't have time for social media or building websites or anything technical. The equine industry has been word of mouth for so many years that social media and the internet didn't impact it until fairly recently.

Also, it's a close-knit community, so trying to get into it is kind of like moving to a small town and trying to make friends. Trying to move into this small niche market and getting into retailers and getting customers is hard—I think it's hard in any industry, but this is an industry in which you have to build a lot of trust before people are willing to take a chance. It isn't an impulse-buying crowd.

Therefore, a lot of our brand credibility came from me being present the first few years and proving myself trustworthy and a reliable resource. Those first couple of years I was really concerned about being rejected and breaking down these barriers. It's an aging industry as well. There are young riders in it, but their influencers are mostly older instructors. Trying to get through to those people and gaining their trust was an uphill battle—I'm not saying that my industry is more difficult than others, but it's not like selling a little accessory or gadget that you can market on social media and it takes off. It's a much more closed-in marketplace. At the beginning, I felt like people were watching me thinking "Who is this company, where did you come from, and no, I don't want to talk to you."

Breaking through these barriers would take a lot of work. I'd have to knock on lots of doors and work like crazy to earn the market's trust. And at that point, I wasn't quite sure how this would happen—but after much trial and error, I learned to make it work. Below are some of the things I figured out along the way—the hard way.

Your Passion Isn't Always Your Customers' Passion

The other thing I didn't realize at first was that **the features of our products that I was most proud of weren't all that interesting to our customers**.

To be honest, I had zero plan for marketing or positioning at first. I went into the marketplace, and there were many things I didn't even think about before I went in. I had zero expectations. I knew the market, but I didn't know it nearly as well as I thought I did, and I had little to no idea of what people were going to want to hear and how to brand the company effectively.

The early feedback from customers about our products was always good, but I didn't have much success attracting new sales. I realized that much of the reasoning behind that was because I was so excited about the science behind our products and how they deliver pain relief (I'd been on a pre-med track in school, and I love science), but **most people are not interested in how something works. They just want to know that it works.**

I can't tell you how many times I would pitch my products—I had a 15-second elevator pitch that I had come up with that would always seem to draw out for more like 45 seconds—people would just walk away, because it was so confusing. I was excited about the therapy and how it worked. So, I would talk about the therapy on a molecular level: what the products were doing, the science behind them, and people would just walk away because they were confused. So really, for the first year of selling, I just watched people walk away (minus the few science buffs who gave me enough sales to keep the company afloat). Slowly I began to understand what people were looking for: the big picture. **People want to know how something benefits them—and you have about 7 seconds capture their attention and deliver that message.** The rare science buffs were different from the people who just wanted to hear the benefits, get the product, and get out. So, it was just a matter of learning who you were talking to.

When I learned that and set my ego aside about the science and all the awesomeness behind the products, I sold a lot more. And learning that changed my business completely, since it meant simplifying things—at least simplifying things to the end consumer in my marketing process. I learned that people only really want to know the core of things. Especially with social media these days, so much is thrown at people, that the faster the better and the quicker you make your point, the better. And I really underestimated that. That was hard for me to accept—but absolutely necessary.

Understanding this also helped me develop an identifiable voice for Benefab®: We're a science-based company, but we're friendly scientists. That means that we want to appear as approachable experts. We like to be friendly, we like to be extremely approachable, we want to be able to teach people, but we're not fun and frills like an accessory or clothing company might be. We've stayed true to that branding strategy. For the first two years, we were all over the place, which I think is understandable—and for most startups—normal. You must keep trying until you find what works for you, but more importantly, your audience and customers. **Facts tell, but emotions sell.**

Now, I no longer have a sales pitch in my head, it's more like a conversation. But there's ten different ways that conversation can go, all with the same objective of closing the sale. That's all it is. From the start of that conversation to the end, it's much more interactive now. It's problem solving, rather than selling. It's delivering solutions rather than delivering products. Once I made that mental shift, the business started to change for the better.

Another thing to remember is the customer's experience is what it's all about in business. It's not about the product necessarily, but the customer's impression of the whole experience—the illusion, if you will. Yes, you need a product that works; you must have a good product. But you also want to create *an experience* for your customer. No matter what, it's the experience that matters the most, so that's what our marketing software and the systems we have in place are doing without us doing it manually: They create that whole experience for the customer.

Your Unique Selling Proposition: "What's in It for Them?"

Another, more challenging part of our branding was **developing our unique selling proposition (USP).** Way too often, people come up with a pitch that doesn't tell people how they'll benefit—and that's the most important part. In today's market, you don't have time to tell people what I refer to as the 5 w's (Who you are, Where you came from, What you do, When you do it and Why). You only have time to say how your product (or service) is going to affect them. **That's critical in developing a USP—how is your product going to affect your customer?** For instance, I think Domino's Pizza's USP is brilliant: "Fresh, hot pizza delivered in 30 minutes or less, guaranteed." It tells you what you're getting, how fast you're getting it and that's it's guaranteed.

I came up with Benefab®'s USP—"Increased mobility and less pain in three weeks, guaranteed"—in a mastermind group. We were talking about USPs specifically while brainstorming about each other's businesses. Our USP tells people what they're getting, which is important. People—okay, except for maybe five percent of them—don't want to know how your products work. Most people just want to know how they're being affected. If you only have a short amount of time or space, don't pitch the features. Pitch the benefits. Everything that we do goes through the USP and the branding: Does it reflect our image as friendly scientists? Is it consistent with our USP of delivering increased mobility and less pain quickly?

Coming up with a strong USP was great for sales. I liked it, and I thought about what it said for about two months after I came up with it. Then I went to a trade show. It was a bit of a bust because it was a new trade show and there weren't a whole lot of people. And it seemed like the people who were there weren't really converting. At this time, we were beginning to be profitable at trade shows, and this trade show was about half of what we were used to doing—we just about broke even.

So, at the next trade show, I thought "You know what? I'm just going to use this unique sales proposition and see if it works." And anytime someone walked into my booth, instead of saying "We offer mineral-infused products that produce far-infrared wavelengths, etc...." I'd welcome them to the booth and say, "With all of our products, we guarantee increased mobility and less pain within three weeks of use. It's our customer promise."

Well, it was amazing—I had hardly any questions about how the products worked, what they were—nothing. It was like the conversions just happened. It was unbelievable, one after another after another after another. It was the biggest trade show I ever had!

Knowing how well our USP converted, we started applying it to our wholesale marketing. We do a fair amount of wholesale, so one thing we had to start doing was put our USP on our packaging, because in wholesale, the products must sell themselves. When you're in a direct sale business, you're controlling the sale, but in wholesale, once that product gets into the store, it must sell itself. This realization started to affect our graphic design work and we started to *imply* the message everywhere—regardless of whether there was room enough to write it.

We've applied this and our brand persona to all our other marketing too. For instance, we do a lot of social media advertising. In our company, we will do a social media graphic, for example. And we will ask ourselves: Is it approachable? Is it engaging? For us specifically and our sales team, are we approachable experts? Is it so science-based that people are intimidated? What I think is a successful tool is old-school: Throw mud at the wall and see what sticks. Modern day translation: put out multiple versions of the same thing and see what gets the most feedback, then run with the one that gets the best response.

Figuring out who we are as a company, who we serve, and what makes us special was key to getting us off the ground. Benefab® had a mission, a brand identity, and great products. But we were still young as a company, and I had a lot to learn.

What Do Your Customers Want? Just Ask.

What we really wanted to do to get feedback was start a conversation with our customers. Understanding our market was one reason why it was so important to listen to our customers. We evolved our product line by listening to feedback and taking into consideration everything that was said. Not that we're necessarily going to do everything our customers suggest, but we take all feedback seriously. That has helped us tremendously along the way. Because in the end, our products are for the customer—this seems obvious, but businesses tend forget that. **Without your customers, you have no business.**

One example of how I learned from our customers had to do with the color and appearance of our products. Color was a big deal to me because I looked at the marketplace and I saw that nobody was making products like ours in colors. Naturally (and naively), I thought this would set us apart.

Colors can be very advantageous to some businesses—I have helped other businesses do very well with color suggestions, but those have been primarily impulse purchases such as inexpensive clothing and accessories. But when I came out with colors, I found through feedback and lack of sales that they weren't well received.

I learned that this decision will completely revolve around your market and your item. Take for example, the iPhone. For years, you could have any color you wanted as long as it was black (it's a joke, you can chuckle). That only changed recently: Apple proved the concept, exceeded sales expectations, and became a trusted name *before* offering colors.

I learned it's best to start with the basics, and once you begin to gain traction, you can add different colors because you then have a built-in, loyal customer base. Through customer feedback and data analysis, we started scaling back on color and offering primarily black and white. We've also made other changes based on customer feedback, which just came down to the tiny details—we've made some of our buckles bigger and done other things to make the products more user-friendly. We've done that almost purely through customer feedback.

We've found social media to be the most scalable way to talk to our customers on a personal wavelength, and that is what's been so important to us. It's given us a platform to be fun and approachable without losing our brand feel—that's incredibly important. The conversation is always continuing on social media. In the past, advertising meant you're on one page of a magazine or heard in one commercial—and potential customers keep flipping the pages and pass your ad before they've had time to mentally absorb the ad material. Social media is helpful because you can be in front of customers consistently. According to CNN.com, people spend on average 10 hours per day using some sort of screen (phones, computers, tablets, TV, etc.). With this sort of statistic, there is no reason why you cannot be in front of your customers one, two, or even five times a day.

With Facebook (and other social media platforms), algorithms have evolved since it began, making it tougher to control who sees your posts and where they show up if you're not sponsoring them with paid placement. But if you do it right, you'll get results—you don't have to be spending hundreds of thousands of dollars a year to be in front of people (even though some companies regularly do). You can get BIG results with a limited budget. It takes trial and error and patience, but it's very doable. Every business is a bit different, but when you find the formula, stick to it! If one thing works, you can translate that into other posts/campaigns to replicate the success.

Many small businesses pay somebody to do social media, and depending upon your business and what you are looking to get out of social media, that may be the right choice. Personally, I don't see social media as a *direct conversion* platform, but instead as a solid lead generation platform with eventual customer conversion. Our social platforms have brought in countless viewers who've eventually converted to paying customers.

One of the most helpful shifts we've made in social media marketing was to look at these platforms as a cocktail party (yes, it's a silly analogy, but hear me out for a second…): If you wouldn't say it at a gathering with friends, you probably shouldn't post it. The idea is to get the customers from that party into "the lounge," whether that's your website, a landing page, or a signup form. That's where you can begin selling and educating, but the party isn't the place to sell.

This has turned into a challenging game for us—we'll do a picture with a blue button versus one with a red button, we'll see what works best and what drives the most traffic and run with the best-performing option. We're always involved in the posts. And you really need to be involved. You must be willing to change frequently and quickly when you see what is and isn't working. That's why I think one of my best moves was to bring our social media in house and do it ourselves, because we know the business better than anybody, and I now have the personnel to manage it. The whole goal for us is generating the **lead generation > engagement > conversion** cycle. With those three things, you can go a long way.

Social media has also helped us reach out to different audiences through targeted marketing. We have a strong wholesale business (B2B), which also helped us gain exposure among potential customers who frequent equine supply shops. We're in shops nationwide that cater to all equine disciplines, so inevitably we're going to be in front of all kinds of people. But marketing to those different subsets was a challenge at first.

For that, we were able to use brand ambassadors in different disciplines—by brand ambassadors, I mean *market influencers*. The brand ambassador program has been fun and rewarding both monetarily and emotionally. Basically, what we do is seek people (at this point, people seek us) who have a large, engaged following on social media. Most who apply are already dedicated users of our products. They're primarily in their late teens or young adult women who have large online audiences and have gone viral one way or another on one or multiple platforms such as YouTube, Facebook, Instagram, blogging, etc. We don't sponsor any of our ambassadors financially, and we require that they be paying customers before becoming ambassadors—we want them to have some skin in the game.

Since we first started this program, it's evolved hugely. At first, we didn't require familiarity with our products for many reasons—a couple worth mentioning are not many people knew about the brand, and frankly, at the time I didn't know better. It felt as if we just got people who wanted free product, but didn't follow through with reviews, posts, and shares.

Now, we have people who are already Benefab® brand believers. They love the products, and basically what they do is they either buy the product for a discount or very occasionally, if they have a great following, they get the product for free. They're required to post about it, talk about it, and share it with their followers and fans. Through their posts, we gain new followers, which leads to new customers because they drop into our cycle (lead generation > engagement > conversion).

To start, I was contacting 1-2 people per week to try my products. Now, we get on average, about 5 sponsorship requests a day. To say the least, we've become much more fastidious about choosing our ambassadors. It's been a successful program, because people see influencers in the industry using our products, which immediately gives the brand added credibility. Plus, there's always a yearning from their followers to be more like them.

Today, thanks to our engagement and research, we have our demographic that we pitch to and we know who our customers are—we know them inside and out.

Expert Tip: Engaging Your Audience

"It is better to go slow in the right direction, than fast in the wrong direction."

This quote by Simon Sinek accurately sums up my thoughts on marketing. It does not matter if you are in the first week, or your tenth year in business, there are foundational principles that go way beyond which social platform you use.

To be consistently great at marketing you have to know your why. You must have a massive passion for the people you plan to serve. You have to be in it for more than just the money. The journey of an entrepreneur is jam packed with a million options and a thousand voices. Your success is found in pinpointing the right option and silencing the voices.

So, how do you find that audience? You have to start with an attractive character. When you have character, integrity, and a dynamite service or product, your vibe will attract your tribe, so to speak. Now, I don't mean customers will magically appear; however, through creative marketing efforts, such as email marketing or a strategic marketing funnel, your audience will come (with lots of hard work, dedication and failing forward).

As that audience grows, how will you communicate with them? What marketing avenues are best suited for your business? These answers are not a one size fits all; however, the foundational principles I mentioned above still apply. Take a moment to think of dating someone new. Typically, you would not ask someone to marry you on the first day, right? How will you get to know them, make them feel special and ultimately get them to buy from you? The answer is looking back at you in the mirror. Bring your unique self always. Remember the Golden Rule. Remember this journey is just that, a journey.

-Jamie Samples
Yellow Barn Media, Founder and CEO
jamie@yellowbarnmedia.com
yellowbarnmedia.com

Competition? What Competition?

What I've learned most along the way is that I'm much better off trying to compete with myself and trying to be the best we can be rather than watching our competitors so closely. I used to be really focused on my competitors: what they were doing and what they weren't doing. I watched them closely (*too* closely). I do believe that you can learn from them, but don't let it become a distraction. Sometimes in marketing, you don't have to reinvent the wheel; you can do things that others in your space are doing successfully and put a unique spin on it for your business. **It's important to watch the horizon, and not let your peripheral vision slow you down.**

It's easy to get sucked in and start comparing yourself to your direct competitors—or for that matter, any success story. The way to really grow is to start being the best that you can be and stop comparing.

We have one direct competitor in my space who was the first to market. We do things a little differently, but the basic idea of wearable wellness is the same. And I used to be laser-focused on what they were doing, and I feel like that slowed me down. Now, I've shifted my focus by thinking, "Okay, let's just be the best we can be and not necessarily watch every move they take. We have our way of doing things and a different personality. We should take advantage of that."

And since I've stopped watching them as closely, my business has grown a lot. We're much more focused on our customer base because we're not as distracted trying to compete with everything they (or anyone else) are doing. We're just competing against ourselves. And because of that, we're going to be bigger and better every day.

I think more than anything, it's the overall customer experience and customer service that makes a business catch fire. We're very involved, we guarantee everything, and we listen to our customers and address things from a solutions standpoint. We care. We're not just selling products. I tell my employees, if the products aren't the right fit, don't try to close the sale.

We really try to market our products to the right customers, and they trust us. It adds a whole other level of credibility when you're able to say, "you know, I don't think this is right for you."

That's not to say we don't want every sale we can close, but I think that mentality does set us apart from a lot of companies, because our customers walk away feeling "they really want what's best for me."

And most of the time, word of mouth starts to trickle down from those people because they do appreciate the sincerity in everything we do. I think it strikes them as refreshing, especially in a noisy marketplace where people are pitched products/ideas/services constantly between social media, email, text, and telephone calls—it becomes exhausting. It's kind of relaxing to meet with someone who doesn't want to pitch, pitch, pitch. We truly want to help.

CHAPTER 4

MISTAKES ARE INEVITABLE

I made a lot of mistakes in the beginning. And I'm sure I'll make more in the future as new challenges arise. But I've learned that what's important is not so much avoiding mistakes, but learning from them when they happen.

For me, a lot of early mistakes just came from inexperience (like choosing that great business name that just so happened to be taken by a multinational company in an overlapping industry). Another early error had to do with ordering from my supplier. When we started, my first order was miniscule. The manufacturer—the gentleman I'd met in Taiwan—said I had to place an order for a thousand pieces of one single product. I couldn't afford that! So, he took a gamble on me and allowed me to place an order for between 30 and 50 pieces of each instead. They used leftover fabric from test runs and other orders, so I had no control over color, material type, etc. But, nonetheless, it was a start!

Anybody who knows anything about textile manufacturing overseas knows that minimums are high—usually a thousand or more of a single product. But they did it because they trusted me, and they wanted my business—they saw an opportunity for themselves. And their gamble paid off; we still do business together today. They were playing the long game and it served them well.

Later, I placed an order for one thousand pairs of polo wraps and a thousand each of two types of saddle pads. We had three thousand pieces on the way (and only three products). Nothing better than that to motivate you to sell, sell, sell!

Some of my mistakes happened because I knew nothing about international shipping and imports. One of the first mistakes I made was shipping the products via air freight, not ocean freight. And I didn't know about the duties—I had no idea about any of that except for what I had read on Google. And I thought,

"My goodness, how am I going to make any money with how expensive the shipping was?"

I later learned that shipping would have been about 30% of what I'd paid had I sent the products via ocean freight. Yes, this takes 35 days versus 3 days, but the savings are far worth the time if you manage it correctly. I had to learn to plan for and expect this.

In my first year of selling those products, I also had a tough time because selling a thousand of one thing is far tougher than I ever imagined it would be. Of course, now, we plan for all this. But at that time, it was just me, and I was renting a small T-hangar at an airport. If I got an order, my whole day stopped, and I'd run down to the airport to pack and ship it.

Having to sell in large quantities meant learning to market our products in a **scalable manner**. Besides having to learn about branding and company image, there were a lot of other things I didn't know. For example, going to that trade show and not knowing anything about trade show setups or how ours should look.

But the biggest marketing mistake I made nearly destroyed the company.

I was approached by a very large magazine publisher. This was a large media group that had multiple magazines under their umbrella. All but one were equestrian-related magazines that catered to what I thought was our target audience. And of course, I was a part of the equine industry, so when I heard the names, I was familiar with them. And the salesperson told me exactly what I wanted to hear. We signed a twelve-month contract—I did negotiate, but it was still a lot of money. Our final contract was roughly $38,000, which is a lot of money for a startup, especially one being run (at the time) by one person. But they had me so convinced me that the return on investment was going to be well worth the cost. That was completely bogus. I did a financing agreement with them, then put out a lot of advertising content that didn't go anywhere. It was a complete loss, essentially—an almost fatal mistake.

And part of the reason for this mistake is there's so much I know now that I didn't know then. First, buying decisions are normally made with the right (emotional) side of the brain, not the left (logical) side. Normally emotional decisions are driven through conversation, stories, pictures, or video—not necessarily text ads. Perhaps if had I used part of that budget towards radio, it may have been a better choice. Would it have been a home run? I don't know. But it probably would have paid for itself.

The second part of my mistake was that at the time, I had a very science-based, educational approach to marketing. But the science can't be explained in one page. So, for me, it was a bad decision to go that route.

It was incredibly draining, not just financially, but emotionally as well. I took a huge risk, put in almost everything I had, and it didn't pay off. There is always risk in any decision (especially marketing) that you make, but that was a bad risk. Looking back—with my experience now, I would never do that. But when you're first starting, you don't know. And if people are promising you rainbows and butterflies and it sounds too good to be true, it probably is. Remember, *unicorns don't exist.*

People tell you what you want to hear. Every business owner wants more sales, more contracts, and more leads. And the marketing agencies know that. Not every marketing agency is bad—there are some great ones out there, but do your homework and listen to trustworthy referrals. Most of the time, referrals are your best business, coming or going.

Most agencies are going to tell you that they can increase your sales, and if you read their contracts, there's of course nothing that guarantees that. You should take things at face value and do your own research. Knowing this hasn't made me gun-shy overall, but I'll tell marketers if they're trying to sell me something, "If you can bring me proof of five customers that this has brought measurable ROI (return on investment) to, then I'll continue the conversation with you." Most never call back because they can't prove it with hard data.

It's not that I'm against all print advertising. Some magazines are still good magazines, and I think sharing stories can be very effective. But in general, numbers and data don't lie. Bring me proof and I won't argue.

I've learned that marketing is like a black hole. I felt that I wasted a lot of money here and there, with the most of my success coming in small increments from trial and error. It's so much more efficient if you start very small and you do it on your own—at least in the beginning. When you've refined your best ideas, find an expert and start to scale. That doesn't necessarily mean hiring an expert through a consultancy firm. I did actually bring on a consultant at the end of my first year because I felt like I was hitting a lot of brick walls. And they helped tremendously with ideas, but there was no plan for *implementation*, so this left me with a lot of material and little funding to act on the ideas.

Most consultants (not all) will tell you what to do and charge you a lot of money for it, but of course, if you don't do it, nothing changes. Most of the time, they tell you what to do but do not put an action plan in place. If you're an entrepreneur, *you* must be the implementer. And hiring those consultants really opened my eyes to that—they did have great ideas that changed my business. **But it was up to me to act and make them happen.**

Doing that print advertising contract was a huge, nearly fatal mistake. Part of the reason I share this with you is not to embarrass myself, but for you to realize that overcoming that hardship was a perfect example of *fast-failing*. Mistakes happen, but how you react to them is imperative. It was terrible, but if I'd sat there for six weeks drowning in my own sorrows, we probably would have gone under. It could very well have been a fatal mistake if I hadn't immediately started searching for everything within my grasp to pull myself out of the hole. And that's when I started considering a third-party distributor and really scaling what I had built.

When beginning my search for distributors, I expanded our trade show routes and implemented a very powerful customer relations management (CRM) software program. This has been tremendously successful in multiplying what I could do by a 1000x per day (literally); we're still using the same program today. It was something that I could implement by myself. Now, my business is working whether my eyes are open or closed. It was a way to scale myself, essentially.

Since the emergence of the internet and the evolution of social media, everyone is changing their way of doing business. As business owners, we must evolve to respond to the technology revolution. It's sad, but a lot of catalogues, Mom-and-Pop stores, and other small businesses are going out of business—if you're not evolving with what the market demands, then you're not going to stay afloat.

So, in the end, this mistake proved to be a way to move the company ahead. And it made me a better business person, more skilled

in negotiation, and more knowledgeable than ever before because it forced me to learn not just how to be the owner of my business—*but the marketer of my business.*

We've coordinated our social media and other marketing copy with our CRM so it all works synergistically—we now do strategic advertising only. In our market, print ads don't convert enough to be worthwhile. Perhaps in another market, it would be completely different—that's where learning and knowing your market is key.

What we've also found is that people like stories—something they can relate to—so we try to share our brand story any way that we can. Emails are a great platform to do that, but you can also do that through articles, media interviews, speaking engagements, blogging and other, more engaged platforms.

Learn to *leverage* your marketing. If you market through **one** media channel, there is no reason that the same ad/article/story cannot be shared on **every** platform. And take time to be sure your piece resonates with your audience and their needs.

Expert Tip: Writing to Sell

You open a text document... Then stare at it... You think, "Where do I start?".

Your fingers are frozen at the keyboard...

I've had this very thing happen to me—MANY times!

One way to get ideas is to ask the following questions:

- *What type of person (or business) am I talking to?*
- *What kind of answers are they looking for?*
- *What frustrations or challenges are they facing?*
- *What specific result (as it pertains to the services I offer) would make their life so much better?*

With answers to these questions, you can begin writing FOR your reader. This is much better than just writing to promote your business. Good copy MUST put the reader FIRST, or it's likely to be ignored.

As copywriters, we must answer (in advance) the questions our readers are asking themselves: "What's in this for me?" "How is this going to help me get the results I need?" "How is this going to improve my life?"

Too many businesses ignore this principle of "giving before receiving" to their own peril. When you speak to your reader as you would to a friend, provide answers they want, and put them FIRST… it is sure to come back to you!

-Seth Hudson
Copywriter & Outdoor Design Expert
LinkedIn https://www.linkedin.com/in/sethhudson/
Get inspiration for your backyard at www.5StepBackyard.com

Risk and Opportunities: When to Take the Leap

Obviously, not every choice you make in business is going to pay off. But for your business to grow, you must take risks.

I love risk—I'm a bit of an adrenaline junkie. But I think that a lot of times risk and opportunity are confused, and it's important to touch on that.

Risk is something that's completely out of our control—when you're driving to the grocery store or getting into your car, you risk getting into an accident. **Opportunity** is something that's within our control—you act to seize an opportunity. So, you can't really take a risk, you take an opportunity and the risk lies within the opportunity.

A lot of times decisions are hard for people to make. We come to this fork in the road, and we tell ourselves whether we should or shouldn't do something. I really struggled with that, like most people, my whole life. When I got into business, the first year, I'd think, "Should we do this? Do we have the budget for it?" as I tried make growth, marketing, and buying decisions.

My belief is **if you can live with the worst-case scenario, go for it.** And that's really what it boils down to. I told myself that if I could live with the worst-case scenario, I should do it. If I'm torn about something, and the worst-case scenario is maybe we'll lose what we paid for something or we'd have extra stock for a while, this was a scenario I could live with. Now, this seems like an obvious way to look at decisions.

Before, I was beating myself up over a lot of decisions—decision-making can be emotionally draining. When I was first selling in stores, I thought, "this is such a risk—what if they steal my idea before patents are granted?" And now I've totally changed my thinking: It's not a risk, it's an opportunity—an opportunity to make a sale. And the biggest risk is that they can say "no."

I've used this in my personal life as well. Even when I was thinking about moving to Florida, I thought, "okay, what if that doesn't work out?" I looked at the worst-case scenario, and the worst-case scenario was I wouldn't like it. And I could live with that. This has become a guiding strategy and mentality in my business.

What's the Worst That Could Happen?

For me, there's a lot of joy in risk. I don't think you can be an entrepreneur if you don't like risk. In my business, the worst worst-case scenario I can recall was ordering some unusual colors in our products—I thought they would go over well, but they didn't work out. So, the worst-case scenario was that I was left with stock that would take a while to sell. And it has sold, but it was a slow drip and there was money tied up in that inventory. So that was one of the times when we lived with the worst-case scenario and we moved on.

Risk tolerance really depends on where you are in your business or personal life. When I was looking to get into business, the worse-case scenario if I'd thrown myself into the business full-time would have been no food on the table. Needless to say, this worst-case scenario was not acceptable, and I kept my day job until that changed. But later, this did become an option: I was at a place where I knew I could start my business full time and live off my savings for quite some time, so I would be okay. That's when I took the leap.

Failure Is Not Permanent (and It's Not Always a Bad Thing)

I think failure is so commonly looked at as a terrible thing, and it's not. I think it should be looked at as a moving state, an evolving process. Failure comes from making mistakes. And you learn from your mistakes.

There's so much pressure to do the right thing, especially for young people—you can't fail this test, you must get A's, you need to make the honor roll, etc. Which are all good things, but we're taught to shy away from failure from a very young age. If you're a child and you knock over your iced tea, that's a "failure," and perhaps your parents are upset. Instead, parents should use this opportunity (or one like it) to explain what the child did to cause the spill (i.e. clumsiness, etc.) so he or she could learn from their mistake. But instead, we often scold them. So, from a very young age, we're programmed to steer away from failure in any way that we can.

But failure is the only way you're going to learn. It's important for people to realize that it's inevitable. You're never going to succeed if you don't fail. There are very few things you can do and succeed at without failing at least one, two, three, four or even five times. It's important for people to hear that because "failure" is often used negatively—it shouldn't be. It simply shows us what we need to work on to succeed the next time.

In any business or life situation, there will be low points and there will be times when you think, "How am I going to pay the bills? How are we going to keep this afloat?" In those moments, you must put one foot in front of the other to keep moving forward, even if you don't know where forward is—just keep making moves! That's one of the most important things—people will crawl into a hole and regress rather than keep moving forward. **That's the key in business—persevering—even if you have no idea what's ahead.**

> *"I do not think that there is any other quality so essential to success of any kind as the quality of perseverance. It overcomes almost everything, even nature." -John D. Rockefeller*

You also should realize there are very few truly overnight successes; you just didn't notice them until they became successful. That's true for singers, song-writers, entrepreneurs, or actresses. Most people have been hanging in there for years before they get their big break. You don't know their stories until you really start researching them. I've read countless stories about founders of some of the most successful companies, and many times they experienced multiple failures before their major successes. In 1923, Walt Disney's first animation, *Alice in Cartoonland*, sent him into bankruptcy. Disney and his partners had a few other failures until his first sound-and-animation production, *Steamboat Willie*, became a success. By 1937, Disney debuted his first full-length film, *Snow White and the Seven Dwarfs*, which, because of the Great Depression, was not expected to do well. But to everyone's surprise, it became the beginning of the brand you and I know today—it was a raging success, but that didn't happen overnight. It took him about 18 years and multiple catastrophes to get there.

Another great example is James Dyson (the founder of Dyson® Vacuums). He worked 5 years and had 5,127 prototypes before succeeding in the creation of a bag-less vacuum! Talk about dedication and failing forward!

So, when you fail or hit a road block, keep marching forward and revising your plan.

Evolve with the current and keep going.

CHAPTER 5

PLANS ARE USELESS
(BUT PLANNING IS ESSENTIAL)

I love the quote by Dwight D. Eisenhower, "Plans are useless, but planning is essential." It's so true—and one of the most important lessons of my life.

You know, I don't think anything ever really goes as planned—business plans and models are often completely useless. When I first started Benefab®, I created an elaborate business plan and listed many ideas (only to impress investors) and realized that half of them never worked out. For instance, I originally planned to promote our line of therapeutic products for people much more strongly, but for various reasons, this turned out not to be feasible financially or logistically. Sales projections don't always become reality, because real life and real markets throw curves nobody can predict in advance. Even my to-do list doesn't always go as planned! I've found that if my plan starts getting in the way of my goals—especially if I've got a goal within close reach—it's time to ditch the plan. But if you don't have a set plan and you don't have a goal in mind, then you're never going to get anywhere because even you don't know where you are going or where you want to be.

You must plan, but you also need flexibility. I can give an example: I had the goal set in stone that I wanted a distributor, and I had four top distributors in my industry that I had been speaking to, and two with whom I would have gone into negotiations and signed on the dotted line. I was so set on those two, and I wanted to work with them, but I just didn't feel we were jibing.

I had the whole thing mapped out—or so I thought. I hadn't written it out step to step, but I had major steps and a timeframe, and we were three months in and none of my options were working to my advantage. After about six months, I was starting to get worried because it was between the two mentioned above—one was a private-equity-type company and I just felt my products were going to sit on a shelf with the other one. But these were the companies I'd listed in my goals.

After a sleepless night, I decided to ditch the plan and shift my focus. I opened my eyes and backed out of those two conversations. Although they had been listed in my original plan, that plan didn't seem to be panning out.

And about that time, I got a lead from somebody who knew somebody else involved in a business that may be a fit. Sound like a long shot? It was, but I made the call.

I ended up speaking with their CEO, and it wasn't all that productive a conversation. I just as easily could have said, "Well, that conversation didn't lead anywhere," but instead I cultivated the relationship and asked, "Do you mind if I fly out to your office to see your operation? Let's just meet, sit down and see if there's any opportunity."

I flew out to their offices, and that was the start of a great business relationship. Their company has therapeutic products and nutraceuticals, so they're science-backed and research-based, like we are. I knew our products weren't going to just sit on the shelf if we worked with them. And most importantly, our brand missions aligned.

In short, I took an interest and it paid off.

Working with a distributor shaves your margins because there's an added middle man who too must be compensated. I had to decide: Was the lesser margin worth it to have a turn-key distribution channel rather than having greater margins but paving those sales channels ourselves, which would take years? They had an already-existing customer base. Not to mention my lack of personnel—we would have to bring in new employees to manage those new accounts and work out the logistics side of things, among other tasks. After weighing the differences, we decided it was worth losing some margin to have that distribution channel.

In each business, people face this same dilemma, whether it's shaving their margins through distribution channels, booking agents, or seeking publishers. The most important question to ask yourself is this: Will the volume produced by this relationship pay back the loss of margins *plus more*?

You make money on margins, not revenues. We can all appreciate the importance of that because the richest man in the world, Jeff Bezos—net worth of $105 billion—says, "Your margin is my opportunity." This is a man who has built an empire on other people's margins.

I think this is a good example of what it means for planning to be essential, even if actual plans aren't. I had a good idea of my plans and my structure, but the original plans didn't pan out. I knew where I wanted to go, but not exactly how I'd get there.

Expert Tip: Funding Your Business

It's been said that entrepreneurship is like jumping off a cliff and creating your parachute on the way down. While it can be terrifying, being in the position of learning so quickly is also one of the things that is so exciting about being a founder.

The feeling of falling from a cliff is certainly how many entrepreneurs feel when they first start raising capital and learning the financial management side of their business. It may seem dry and uninteresting to some, but without that financial health, the goal of why you started your business to begin with can't be realized. It therefore makes it one of the most important things for you to learn as a new entrepreneur.

If you want to create a startup with the goal of growing large and nationwide or even global very quickly, you will likely also be raising capital from investors. This has become exceptionally popular with shows like Shark Tank, with entrepreneurs thinking they need to immediately find angel investors.

However, entrepreneurs need to understand that investors need an "exit," which means that they need to get their cash back with a large return one day (their target is a 10x return). This is often in the form of selling your company in an acquisition, but can also mean your company goes public onto the stock market or some other more complicated arrangement. The moment you take money for equity in your company, you are agreeing that you will get those investors an exit one day.

This might not be the best fit for everyone. If you want a business to support yourself and your family, or you want to have a service business where you have clients, you will likely want to turn to other sources of capital, so you don't have that commitment of an exit.

Even if you do want to raise money from angel investors, they want to see proof that your idea will work. In other words, they want you to already have traction, such as users, sales revenue, or other evidence that people want your product or service!

The good news is that there is a variety of ways to raise capital to get to that point, and of course it's important to understand the commitments that come with each one.

- Crowdfunding — platforms like Kickstarter allow individuals (the crowd) to commit money to a concept that is not yet created. Money you raise here is treated much like pre-order revenue, and if you reach your funding goal, you will commit to make it happen and communicate with your backers.
- Grants — A variety of grants are available, with some of the most popular for technology companies being the Small Business Innovation Research (SBIR) grants, which between Phase I and Phase II can provide around $1 million in funding, without requiring you to give away any ownership of your company.
- Friends & Family — This is often where entrepreneurs start, and unlike professional angel investors, they may agree to just get their money back (instead of a 10x return), so it can be a great option as long as you are clear with them about the risks.
- Loans — More traditional forms of lending are often overlooked because of the risks involved in new ventures, but if you feel confident in being able

to pay it back personally or already have sales pending and just need some help getting there, this can still be a great option.

- *Services/Consulting — While this can slow down your progress on a product you want to sell, some people offer services or consulting in their (or their team's) area of expertise and put the profit from that back into development of their core business.*

In my own business, we've done all of the above, including raising funds from angel and professional investors who expect a return. Definitely take the time when you get started to consider fully what is best for your business and your goals, because everyone's needs are different!

-Lindsey Tropf
Immersed Games, Co-founder and CEO
www.immersedgames.com

Another big change in planning was the actual growth of our product line. After I started Benefab®, I realized I had to not only expand, but shift the kind of products we offered. I have competition, like every business does— many therapeutic products for horses and people are already available in the marketplace. Business was growing steadily, but I wasn't pleased with the growth rate. And what we really needed was a core differentiator that set us apart in a visible way, because our special mineral-infused fabric just looks like regular fabric.

We've cultivated a lot of trust, and our clients trust our products and believe in their benefits. We also have clinical studies that endorse the validity of the science behind our products. But there was nothing unique that people could touch and feel (other than the fabric), and people absolutely love to touch and feel things. We wanted to have something tangible as a differentiator.

I began looking for this core differentiator, and I wanted it to be something that people could see. I did a lot of research, and I came up with the idea of using magnets because they're used in ancient Chinese medicine—which is already the foundation of our products. In ancient Chinese medicine, acupuncturists take your own blood and redirect it over acupuncture points. Our medical-grade magnets pull the blood closer to the magnet which is strategically pre-sewn over acupuncture points, replicating a less invasive, wearable form of acupuncture.

Our new, SMART products place magnets over predetermined acupuncture points; it's a more targeted therapy and it's also something people can *see*. And this has tremendously grown the business.

This was one of those situations in which I could have hung steady, doing what I was doing—but instead it became a prime example of finding something else and growing from what we had without getting away from our core values. It let us add a whole other element and a whole other stream of income without getting away from why we were originally in business. It didn't change my branding, it enhanced it, and it didn't steer us away from our original philosophy and core values. *It scaled my business.*

I see a lot of businesses that are struggling, and they shift away from their original focus—compromising their brand image. When you do this, you then have a customer base who feels left behind—they were there for your original focus, and now they are not getting what they signed up for. I think we did a really good job of keeping our original customer base happy while enhancing the brand for them and also building an entirely new customer base.

Distraction or Opportunity? How to Spot the Difference

I heard Terry Brock of *Achievement Systems* speak once—and he said, "look out for distractions disguised as opportunities." And I've found this to be true. Many times, I see a potential opportunity, and I think to myself "that would be a really good idea, but is it going to affect me or my business right away?"

That's how I filter things: I look at an opportunity overall and think, "Is it going to affect my customer's experience? Is it going to grow my sales? Is it going to grow the brand altogether?" Because that's the ultimate answer. Brainstorming with other people is helpful too. Sometimes you need to speak with a trusted, reliable resource to come to a decision.

For instance, one of the things I considered was re-launching and heavily promoting our people product line. We sell therapeutic products for people as a companion product to the animal lines, which limits our reach in the human marketplace (considering we only market these products to animal owners who are existing customers). To capture and influence the people market effectively, you need a multimillion-dollar marketing budget simply because the market is so large. We would no longer be in a niche market-place. And of course, for our products to make any sort of medical claim, we would need structured clinical trials for our products to go through FDA approval as medical devices. That's a time-consuming and financially demanding process, which we know well, since we've navigated that same path on the veterinary science side.

There is a huge *opportunity* because the potential market is so large. Spending in alternative over-the-counter therapies is huge ($33.9 billion in 2015). We had to consider whether it was worth a multimillion-dollar investment and the amount of time (likely three years if you worked quickly). I still struggle with this decision daily, but I've decided it would be much more worthwhile for the business to go into another niche market with more opportunity for scalabil-ity—the canine and feline markets—than to try to tackle the people product market. Plus, we are great at what we do and I'm passionate about animals, so it's a perfect fit.

The equine market we obviously do fully, and we plan to launch the canine and feline lines in 2019. That's very new for us. And this reinforces the need to have laser-like focus—I can't launch the canine products and try to relaunch the human line, either financially or logistically. You can't be spread so thinly. I had to choose one, and the canine market is much more manageable—unfortunately, money doesn't grow on trees and I can't come up with a million dollars to push the people line quickly. And without scaling it quickly, it simply wouldn't pay off.

Strategic decisions are made by weighing the risk and the reward. I don't think there's a wrong decision. I think a lot of times in decision making, there's not necessarily a wrong decision, but once you decide, you've got to run with that decision. I don't believe there was a wrong decision in this situation ei-ther—it was just which decision was affordable, going to pay off more quickly, and perhaps be simpler. **Remember, you are better off making a wrong decision than no decision at all.**

Negotiation: Planning for the Unplannable

Negotiation is another big area in which you can't always have set plans—in any given negotiation, there's no telling how things will work out. But it's important to go in with a clear strategy and vision of what you want and what you can accept. It was once said, that if you're buying at an auction, you must know your price, and be willing to walk away if it goes beyond that. In many ways, negotiations are the same.

I was lucky because the first negotiation I was ever involved in was when I was 12 years selling a pony. From age 12 to 16, my parents were involved in helping me buy and sell horses. At age 16, I started doing it on my own (with funding from my father).

I'll never forget the first pony I sold on my own—his name was Aladdin, and I negotiated the whole deal: the buy price and the sale. That transaction gave me the confidence of knowing I could do this on my own. Many years have passed since then and the numbers have grown significantly, but not really the techniques—you learn to get better and better.

Whether selling a business, negotiating manufacturing prices, or negotiating a licensing agreement, you need to know your limits: Know your price and when you will walk away—you need go in with the mindset of what you want. It's like going to an auction—if you want something at market price, you don't go to an auction and say, "I want that, and I'll keep bidding until I get it!" *Especially if you're planning on re-selling that something.* You go in and know the price you'll pay, and if it goes above that, you walk away. Otherwise, you find yourself upside down and not able to recoup your investment. It's the same but reversed in negotiation. You must know your bottom dollar, and if you can't get that, you must be willing to walk away. If emotions become involved, you will likely overpay. For sellers, that's the perfect buyer.

If you're willing to walk away and do walk, I think that puts you in a better place, because people respect that. It also gives you an upper hand because it shows you're strong and you don't need that deal.

Another powerful tool is **silence**. For one, people will tell you a lot of things because most people don't know how to deal with silence. Secondly, if you're negotiating a deal, there is nothing that can go wrong from you staying silent and giving yourself time to think—that's important.

If someone is negotiating aggressively or rushing you, fine, there's probably not much in that deal for you, anyway. For women especially, it's easy to feel pressured. By being silent, people will respect you and it will give yourself time to think and stay grounded. The powers of silence are huge, in negotiations, in sales, and overall. **Don't be afraid of silence.**

Practical Planning

Being committed to planning is the only way to keep on track, especially when things get busy.

I try to stay focused by writing everything down—everything! I am an organizational queen, even though my desk doesn't look like it. Prioritizing has been huge for me, and every day, I have a daily to-do list. I also have a master to-do list. My master to-do list stretches out to the end of the year and is written in a goal-setting format. For example, I write the task with a deadline such as:

"I will have_____ by _____."

So, it's a goal-setting format rather than just "do this, do that." If you just saw those blanks and felt encouraged to write something, do it. This is the perfect time to start.

My daily list is for the general tasks—checking off the boxes. Writing down your goals is critical to your success. It's extremely important in general, but I also think being able to refer to that master list and frequently seeing my goals in writing plays a vital role in achieving those goals.

Eventually it becomes a belief about yourself, not just a goal.

I also find it helpful to have a pattern to my workdays. For instance, when I get into my office, I reply to all my emails, sift through paperwork, and start implementing the steps to achieve my daily and long-term goals. **But, I also try to set aside one day a month to use as a purely creative day.**

I first heard of this idea from serial entrepreneur Dan Kennedy, who talked about it on a podcast. Sometimes I try and do this more than once a month—I try to turn off everything that's going on in my mind and think outside the box.

This is useful because on most days, I get tied up with the small stuff of day-to-day operations. A creative day gives me the freedom to look at the big picture and get a bird's-eye view of the happenings not only in my business, but in the industry and other related fields. This gives me an opportunity to recognize holes that need to be sealed as well as discover new opportunities. For instance, many times, I try to envision myself as a customer and ask myself "What makes this product something I can't live without?" This question alone has spurred a lot of creativity in our marketing campaigns as well as in new product development.

My public speaking is a big part of my professional plan that developed from one of those days. So, these days are for thinking of ways to be creative, to scale the business, and to get outside of the box.

It's been helpful. It's easy as an entrepreneur to start seeing only what's in front of you because you're bogged down with the day-to-day stressors. Setting time aside really allows you the time to take a deep breath and look at things from a broader perspective. Creative days simply create the distance to think with more clarity and creativity.

Systems and Automation—How to Save Time as You Grow

As Benefab® grew, I realized I couldn't do everything alone—not well, anyway. With this realization, I began putting systems and people in place to leverage myself.

Having job descriptions and good leadership has been crucial to my employees' success. It's also been helpful for me. Each person has a task that they handle, and they know it inside and out. This has really helped the company become a small, well-oiled machine. When you put certain people in charge of certain things and you delegate responsibly and wisely, it allows for much more control on a branding level. It means you can deliver a more cohesive message to your customers more frequently.

Marketing takes up a massive amount of time. I used to feel that unless I was at my computer, physically working on my customer base, I wasn't selling the product. I knew that wasn't scalable in the long-term, so I began researching systems that could develop and grow that customer base for me without me sitting at my computer. Then I implemented an automated system that would let me gather customers while I sleep.

There are a lot of automated marketing platforms available, but I decided to go with a high-powered, highly intelligent, customer relations management software program that can run multilevel campaigns all while tracking customer behaviors. That system changed my business completely. It personalizes emails that I already set in place. It also allows me to generate leads without necessarily having to create the lead myself. How it works is first, we create a web form that can collect any customer information we want—first name, last name, email, phone number, what they were interested in buying—whatever information we choose to request.

Next, when a person submits that web form, they're dropped into a campaign. And that campaign would depend on where we wanted that person to go—say, they signed up to learn about horse products. They'd be dropped into a horse product campaign, and they'd be in my system for 24 months (or for however long that campaign lasts), and the system would automatically send them information about our horse products. I never have to do anything except initially set up that campaign or respond if someone replied to an auto-generated email. You can customize their experience—if they click one place, they could be steered elsewhere and dropped into another, more customized campaign, and so on and so forth. It's a custom experience that I don't have to manage one person at a time.

So that freed up a lot more time, because before that, I'd been using a different system that would just notify me, "a person clicked here; you should send them an email," so I would go in and email them manually. Now I don't have to write any emails unless they're fully custom. We can now automatically track everything—they made a purchase, they landed on a page—we can customize the experience for each of the thousands of customers we have, and each one is getting a different experience. We have about thirty different campaigns, so depending on where that customer clicks or where they signed up or how they chose to learn about us, all that information determines what campaign they're dropped into, so it's a customized experience—they're only going to learn what they want to learn about. Someone who signed up to learn about our socks isn't going to get an email about a horse blanket.

There's no one solution that works for everyone. There are less-powerful CRM platforms such as Insightly or email platforms like MailChimp that work for people on smaller budgets. You should do ample research, find systems and planning mechanisms that work for you, and be willing to stick with them. And don't be afraid to change things around as your business evolves—because it will!

CHAPTER 6

IT'S ALL IN YOUR HEAD: HARNESSING THE POWER OF THE MIND

Growing up, I was taught that our mind is so much more powerful than we realize. My grandmother was very influential in my early life. She passed away when I was only 11, but she used to tell me that she introduced my dad as "Dr. Chrysostom" when he was a child, and he's a doctor today.

For me, I've learned that if I really want to put my mind to something, I must believe that "something" will happen—more so than believing, *I envision it*. For example, when I was planning this book, I was thinking and referring to myself as an author before I was published.

Knowing what you want and truly believing it will transform that want into reality. **Our perception is our reality.** When I go into a meeting and I know there's going to be negotiations, I envision a shield of armor on me. I know this sounds silly, but it strengthens my mind and it works—for me, it acts as a mental shield. Our brain is a muscle—you can work it and begin to realize how powerful you can be aside from just your known strengths and weaknesses: What you want and what you envision are what you'll get.

I'm a big believer in the Law of Attraction—the idea that what you think about is what's attracted to you—and I have a very strong mind and a very strong will. When I was young, I thought like that. But when I went to high school and college, like most other people, the distractions came, and the world kind of convinces you that it's not true—for some people, the Law of Attraction does seem farfetched. I'm a science nerd, so I understand that perspective, but envisioning your goals is the most important part of your success.

When I got into business, I started to realize you have to persevere, you must have a strong will, you must have the mindset to move forward, and you must envision yourself where you want to be—that's the key. Anyone who's skeptical about the Law of Attraction should talk to anyone who's successful—they'll find most, if not all, successful people use it in one way or another, and they'll quickly become believers.

I can think of several cases when the Law of Attraction worked for me. For a time, I needed someone to help me with sizing and the overall construction of our products. During this time, I was giving lots of presentations—I just wanted to put myself out there and share what Benefab® was doing. I didn't even voice this need for help, I just kept thinking about it. And yes, it was on my list of goals.

During one of the first presentations I did, a technical designer was in the audience. At that time, I didn't even know technical design was a field, but these people literally specialize in the sizing and overall construction of textile products. So, after a formal interview, I hired her.

Another area in which it helped me was public speaking, which has also become one of my passions. When I began speaking, I was a nervous wreck. Most of my past speaking experiences were with somebody else, so there was always a backup. But my first solo public speaking event was a simple thank-you. It was in Taiwan—thank God most of the audience didn't speak English, because it was horrible! I was shaking like a leaf, and it was probably only two minutes long, but it felt like eons. There were only a few people in the room who could speak English fluently, and after my speech, one of them came up to me—I'll never forget it—and he said in this strong accent, "You know, Kat, speeches are a lot like miniskirts—the shorter the better." And I thought, "Well, that was a nice way of saying, 'it stunk!'"

After that, I decided I needed to join Toastmasters, a global speaking club that empowers members to develop communication and leadership skills. I thought that as this business grew, I would have to be in front of people, so improving my communication skills was a must.

I found a club to join, and the first time I attended the meeting as a guest, there was a speaker who's still part of our club—he's an active member who's great at speaking. I'd been to marketing conferences and such, but this was the first speaker that I'd seen who was really good. His presentation was short, but

. Somehow, he was able to convey a powerful message in a clear,
he only spoke for a few minutes, but I thought, "I want to be able
to   shortly thereafter, I went to a marketing conference, and saw another spe.. er who was even better—and I knew that was what I wanted to speak
like. It was another *opportunity*.

From then on, I really envisioned myself speaking to audiences and becoming the person on the stage. I've since won a handful of awards for speaking, and
that goal is coming to fruition.

Speaking is a fabulous platform for sharing your story and ideas in a scalable
way, just as videos and social media are. But it's far more personal than watching
a screen, so your message can really resonate with people. I'd like to use public
speaking to share my story through inspirational and educational messages—of
course, my products are naturally a large part of my journey, so they are always
incorporated in one way or another. For me, it's about delivering people the
tools to live the life they want and realize success.

What this process taught me is you must know where you want to be to get
there. Write it down, but more importantly, believe it. If you want a specific
amount of money in your account, try to envision that number on your bank
statement. Or if your goal is to win an award, envision yourself holding that tro-
phy. The first step is to know your goals and very specific aspects of that goal, so
you have something to envision. And then you must be open to opportunities as
they present themselves. If you know what you want but you're sitting inside all
day, not opening yourself to new experiences, people, and opportunities, you're
not going to go far. Someone once said, "It's not enough to know where you're
going, you have to hoist the sail."

Cultivating an Entrepreneurial Mindset

Learning to see the world like an entrepreneur is also important for getting a
new business off the ground. I was lucky in that I grew up with this mindset,
since my dad was an entrepreneur who had built a successful business. I have
carried the lessons I was raised with into my business.

I also have learned how to face challenges like an entrepreneur. When I was twelve years old, I saw a pony at a horse show and I just loved it; it was beautiful and talented. And when they told me the price: $15,000—it was clearly out of our price range.

I was only 12, but that pony sparked something in me—I was going to get that pony, no matter how we made it happen. I remember having the conversation with my mom and dad, and they were totally closed to that idea. But I was so strong willed my parents rarely succeeded in telling me "no."

I think this too was an important early lesson—**"no" is not the end of the road.** About three weeks after that initial conversation with my parents, I learned the owners were having a hard time selling him, so I thought *maybe* we could make it happen. (The pony's name was Bucky, which is an honest description of what he did—he bucked everybody off.) His trainer—probably in her late 40s—was the only person who was able to successfully ride him.

One day, Rose Marie, my trainer, surprised me by picking me up early from school and taking me up to the barn where Bucky was stabled—but I didn't know it at the time. I got out of the car, curious as to what we were doing. I saw Bucky in a stall and lit up—we were there to try him!

So, I rode him. I'm sure they were all thinking, "this child won't leave us alone about this pony, so let's take her, it will probably go badly, and she will be quiet."

But it went really well—*really, really* well, and I cried all the way home. I remember Rose Marie saying in her high-pitched tone, "Oh child, I thought you were going to go up there, and it was going to be no good, so you'd be quiet about it!"

I got home, and I told my parents how well it went. And long story short, about three days later, I still couldn't accept that he wasn't going to mine. I bargained, but unfortunately mowing the lawn and cleaning the dishes for a year wouldn't add up to $15,000. But I went out to the barn later that week, and Bucky was in the paddock!

It turns out my dad had negotiated the sale price down to $2,500 because they couldn't sell him. And I kept that pony for a year. Together, we qualified for our regional pony finals, which was a big deal at the time. This had been my goal as a child rider, and it was my last year on ponies because I was outgrowing them—I was getting too tall and was ready to move on to horses.

I ended up winning the Finals that year. I've always had a competitive edge, but that was the first time I experienced that *winning* feeling, and I always wanted to replicate it. That was my first big business break, if you will. We ended up doing very well with that pony when we resold him; we set a lot of that money aside for my schooling. This was the beginning of my life as an entrepreneur.

I was fortunate to have grown up with the mentors and resources I had, and I know not everyone is that lucky. But the main takeaways I've carried with me are those that anyone can embrace to start thinking like an entrepreneur:

- **The power of persistence**. There's truth in the old saying, "don't take 'no' for an answer." Remember that "no" sometimes just means "not yet" or "not this way." So, keep pushing for what you want, and keep conditioning your mind to always look past "no" to the potential for "yes."
- **The power of passion.** To attain a difficult goal, you must want it badly— really badly. Badly enough to work nights and weekends for it (or, in the case of my tween experience, badly enough to nag my dad relentlessly about it for weeks on end!) The reality is things will get tough when you're starting a business, and to keep going, you need to keep that fire alive.
- **The power of accountability.** Learning to track my expenses and keep up with my end of the bargain—like helping to care for our horses—was an important lesson for me. Remember, when you're an entrepreneur, the buck stops with you—hold yourself accountable in everything you do.

Embracing Who You Are: The Challenges of Being a Woman Entrepreneur

It's also important to embrace who you are and how you relate to others. In my case, being both young and a woman entrepreneur has been both advantageous and disadvantageous. Before you open your mouth, you're already judged. I am not a feminist; I think men and women are equal and we should be treated equally (and in most cases, we are). I believe that women have a huge advantage in running a business, because first, we pay more attention to details to prevent problems; and second, we connect much more easily with people emotionally, which is really important for the face of any business.

But it's also a double-edged sword because, as women, we have a hard time making decisions due to the way we're emotionally wired, so it can be very hard to cut off something that needs to be stopped and to do it promptly. This is especially hard if you have developed any level of relationship with the person involved. For example, say you hired an independent contractor for marketing who is working hard with the best of intentions, but not delivering the expected ROI. For women, and sometimes men, this can get sticky because emotions become entangled—we like them, they're nice, they're trying hard, etc. Whether you're a man or woman, if you find yourself in this situation, take the emotions out of it (the grey area, if you will). Look at the black and white: *Are they doing what they promised and is it making money?* If the answer to one or both is *NO*, put an end to it and move on.

In the very beginning, if I went to an important meeting, I would bring my partner, because having a man seemed to automatically bring a bit of credibility. But beyond that, it was for his professional advice. Now, I attend almost all events, presentations, and meetings alone—with confidence.

As humans, we can become ungrounded under pressure and begin spiraling into anxiety. Whatever the discussion and circumstances might be, I've found that being present and slow to speak has really helped me. If you demand respect, not through begging but through action, knowledge, and experience, you will be respected. A great excerpt from Steve Forbes' letter to his subscribers said "Who is the most interesting person in the room? He or she isn't the wittiest, the most attractive, or the one whose reputation precedes them. The most interesting person in the room is the man or woman who easily commands a wide range of knowledge. Who confidently moves the conversation forward with a little-known fact or insight..." Knowledge is power; power boasts confidence.

I don't think the challenges are different for men and women, but I think their perspectives are different. I think a single, young female walking into the Silicon Valley is very different than a single, young male. Tech startups are very male-oriented. It depends on where you are in the world and what you're looking to do. But more than anything, your preparedness and communication skills are what will propel your success.

Also, balancing work and personal life can be tough for a lot of women—especially those with children.

At first, I worked around the clock with little to no traction, which is emotionally draining. It's still challenging, but I have such passion and love for what I do that it doesn't feel like work to me. Plus, the reward of customer testimonials rolling in along with orders far outweighs the workload.

If I need to get away, I also have systems and delegation in place so that I can go visit my family and friends or have a getaway alone for a few days and not have to worry how the orders are going to get out or emails be answered. As you implement systems and structure, try to slowly work toward enabling your business to run while you're away. It's not an overnight transition—I'm still not there, but we're well on the way.

I think honestly, in the startup stage, whether it's a medical practice, a restaurant, storefront, or online business, you must be there to put the systems in place, run it, recognize holes and fix them. You have to know what's happening, perfect the process, and become the marketer of the business—until you get to that point, your business needs you 100 percent. Obviously, you need to have some balance for your sanity. Even if it's one day a week, try to set aside a few hours for yourself—read a book, enjoy a walk, do yoga—something to relax. Those small things make a big difference.

Yes, I do work a lot, but I set personal time aside. I'm not a social butterfly who goes out a lot, but the friends I do have are close friends. And I make it a point to call them regularly and keep these relationships active. When they call me, I answer.

I also like to be alone. And I think that really helps me in regard to balance. In the morning, I have quiet time. I'll read a devotional and spend 30 minutes making my coffee, loving on my dog, and thinking about the day ahead. Also, being active helps—I love to walk and ride my horse. Being part of nature is a huge balance for me, being in fresh air. Find what makes you relax and set time aside for that activity. When you lose that, you're losing quality of life. Everyone is guilty of that from time to time, but keep it in check, because what's everything worth if you can't enjoy it?

The Value of Rejection

Sometimes, you've got to keep going even when doors keep getting slammed in your face. It's important to be persistent, even when it's uncomfortable, because being forced out of your comfort zone is what makes you grow.

Of the things that used to be uncomfortable for me, the first that come to mind are trade shows and cold calls. And when I cold called, this meant walking into a store, not just picking up the phone, because on the phone people can hang up before you even finish your first sentence.

We have a competitor in our space, the wearable therapy space, and they were the only game in town for a long time. And by in town, I mean the industry. They were the only company who was making similar products before we came along. That was hard for us because they've been in business for decades, so they are deeply integrated in the equine industry. So everywhere I went to sell my product, I heard the question "What makes your products different?"

That was difficult to answer, and I honestly floundered, not knowing quite what to say. We had better quality, more features—I came up with a thousand different reasons, and I truly cannot tell you how many times I heard that same question. And it was good for me because it made me not fear rejection and ultimately made me a better communicator. Now, when I walk into speak with a potential buyer, "no" just ricochets off me. **I don't** *sell products* **anymore, I** *provide solutions.* **Because of that, I'm no longer a pesky salesperson, I'm a welcomed guest.**

And it was the same thing at the trade shows. I'd hear the exact same question. It wasn't like I woke up one day and thought "Hey, here's the magic answer to that question!" Instead, it was a steady progression to develop and perfect my answers. *I kept doing it*—that's how I got better.

Curious what that *magic* answer is? We go on the *offense* rather than on *defense*. That is something that's been very helpful for me because when you go on the defense, defending your product against a competitor, they're still thinking about your competitor, and your competitor is still the topic of that conversation. And you also may not realize it, but when you focus on your business and not your competitors, your body language changes, you're no longer defensive and you're in control of the conversation. So now we say, "We're not an expert on what they do—but here's what we do best…"

It's amazing how well people receive that answer, and that started to change things for me—this was when I started getting more distributors seeking us and we started seeking them, and that's when the real growth and evolution of our brand began.

For the first two years, I'd literally sit in my trade show booth and wonder "What am I doing here?" And I think that's where perseverance came in. A lot of people try to get into a space and they give up, they run out of money or patience, but our persistence paid off.

Having those doors shut forced me to learn. And it made me overcome my fear of rejection. Why many people are so afraid of doing something is because of the fear of being rejected, which is something you can't overcome until you just get out there and do it, over and over and over again. Then you realize that you're back to the worst-case scenario—can you live with somebody saying "no" to your face? Of course, you can!

Keeping the Passion Alive

When you find your purpose—your why—the money will come. I often think back to one of the first Benefab® users: My own horse, Papa, who was suffering from a chronic illness that was extraordinarily aggressive. He was in a lot of pain and he had become so defensive that approaching him was difficult—even his skin hurt. But I was his person. He trusted me. Every day, I would use my products on him, and you could see the relief in his eyes when I laid the therapeutic blanket across his back. His facial expressions would soften, and he would begin to lick and chew (something that horses do when they relax, as the chewing motion naturally releases dopamine). Months passed, and sadly, his body had turned against him, and the day came where I had to make the most difficult decision of my life—one that held his life, so delicately, in my hands. As I approached him to say our final goodbyes and hold him during his last moments, he looked at me and began to lick and chew.

As I recall that day, my throat becomes tight and my vision blurs. I often say if something makes your face get hot, your heart start to beat a little harder or your hair stand up on the back of your neck, that's passion—that's what it's all about.

Every week, someone or some situation reminds me of my purpose and the passion that so strongly follows that purpose. But Papa was the spark that lit that flame—and he is ultimately the reason I do what I do.

For me, if I'm just having a bad day, it's best for me to just get out of my office and go ride, which helps me unwind—maybe for you, its gardening or some other activity. Even if I'm too tired to ride, I'll just go and spend time with the horses—something to refocus my mind.

Sometimes, after long days and late nights, it's hard to keep feeling passionate about what I'm doing. But I'm convinced that if you're not enthusiastic about what you're doing, your work isn't going to be good. And this means you must stay enthusiastic, no matter what.

I've learned that if I'm not in a good mental state of mind, I just won't work on complex issues, because it's better that way—if you've ever hit the "send" button on an email when you were in a bad state of mind, you know what can happen!

One way I've kept my passion strong is by always remembering why I'm doing what I'm doing. For me, everything I'm doing now—like speaking and my main business, Benefab® by Sore No-More®—is all about helping people and animals. It's important to be able to recognize your purpose, especially during hard times. At low points, I think that's what really keeps me going, and that's my *why*. I can say that even if I have an unhappy customer or I'm having a personal low point, I'm still doing what I want to do, which is to help people and animals feel their best—that's what keeps me enthusiastic.

Another thing that helps me tremendously during these times is my faith. I grew up a Greek Orthodox Christian and was baptized Greek Orthodox. Religion was always a part of my life; we went to church every Sunday, but it wasn't necessarily the priority it should have been. In high school, I got more involved with Young Life—a Christian teen group—and became much stronger in my faith. When I went to college, I think I did what most young people do and got a bit distracted, which is normal—not necessarily okay, but normal.

Later, when the business started to take off, I left New Hampshire and moved back to Ocala. There, I got back involved in the church. I now have a deeper faith than ever before, and that lingering darkness from the accident has since turned to light.

Another thing that keeps me going is celebrating the small successes. I think that's something that can easily be lost when you're so concerned about getting to the bigger victories. But, if you don't celebrate your small victories, when will you celebrate? You should appreciate the moments when things go well—even if they're small.

The ability to take on big goals comes from simply making a list that breaks that big goal into manageable steps. And then when you complete each of those smaller steps, reward yourself. Celebrate everything along the way. This is helpful because it keeps your enthusiasm—you stay positive much more easily when you're able to celebrate the small successes.

The little wins are just that—small victories that keep you moving forward. For me, examples of small victories would be booking a speaking engagement, landing a new retailer, maybe getting a catalogue to carry my products—it's not such a big thing, but each piece adds to your success. Being able to appreciate these things helps make this entire journey more worthwhile. When the bad things happen, they happen. The bad is as much a part of this journey as the good (in some cases, the bad plays a bigger role). But for the most part, if you celebrate every small success, you're going to be celebrating a lot.

Celebrating these wins means giving yourself permission to enjoy a little reward, like going and buying a new outfit or going out to a nice dinner. Treat yourself—go buy yourself a latte at Starbucks, sleep in one day—whatever it is, reward yourself. If you're not rewarding yourself, then what's in it for you?

I think having those small successes and remembering them will make your load a little lighter, whatever it is you're going through. But generally speaking, just keep going. If things get rough, accept how you feel and begin searching for opportunities to work your way out of the rough tide. If you feel stuck, then pick up the phone—call somebody who might be able to lend you some advice. No matter what, keep moving forward. Even if you don't know where forward is going to lead, take steps. Staying stagnant will only get you more stuck. Acting right away is key.

Finally, you must have a sense of humor. You can't take yourself or life too seriously—you're not the only one who matters. When you want to cry, perhaps laughing is a better option. You must keep your enthusiasm—and if you're truly passionate about what you do, you're not going to become burned out.

There have been many times when I've opened an email from someone who was asking for or suggesting something irrational—so you've just got to have a sense of humor about your network and remember you're dealing with a big range of humanity. To each their own—it's all part business.

In short, if you're in business just to make money, you probably shouldn't do it. When I first started this, that was my goal for the first year. And really, until I experienced the personal benefits of the far-infrared therapy and had other people come to me in tears saying how much it helped them, I didn't develop the passion for what I do as strongly as I have now.

It's no secret: for the first year, business wasn't good. But now I think my passion shines through to the end customer, and people want to do business with us because of that. My passion and our company mission flows through to every level of the business—employees, vendors, and last but certainly not least, my customers.

It is important to help people along the way by giving your product to charities or helping the planet in whatever capacity you are able—to contribute to something in some way. Right now, giving back for me means sharing my story and supporting people on their life journeys. I don't have the secrets to success; nobody does, and if they say they do, they're lying. But I can surely give people tools to use along the way, and I believe that's part of my purpose—I want people to feel that they are amazing, and they can do things they set their mind to—you have as much an opportunity as almost anyone else. Inspirational messages are… well, inspirational—but most of the time it stops there. I want people to know that they are amazing and can do what they want. I want to give them tools to shape the life they want and take control of that life. That's most important in everything that I do—helping people by giving them mental tools to move forward, helping them create some sustainability.

So, for me, part of moving forward is giving back. The world is changing, and people really appreciate good deeds.

But How Can I Be Passionate if I Don't Have a Passion?

People often say, "I don't know what my passion is." I didn't either, until I started Benefab®. Obviously, I was always passionate about horses and I'm still passionate about them, **but my accident stripped me of my core identity, leaving me powerless and lost.**

I developed my newfound passion for entrepreneurship during that time—with a whole lot of determination and fight. Finding your passion is not like shopping for that perfect outfit. To find your passion, you must get yourself out there and have new experiences—you're not going to find passion by sitting back and reading about things. Passion means hands-on experience.

Some of the most successful small business owners that I know developed passions they didn't even know existed just through experience. They stumbled upon something and found that they loved it. For instance, I met a gentleman at a trade show whose wife had kidney failure, and after many failed medical treatments, they began researching holistic remedies. Because of their research, they started infusing her water with different herbs and fruits, and she got her medical condition under control. This sparked a passion! As a team, they invented a water bottle that allows you to infuse herbs and fruit through an encasement in the bottle's core—now their business feeds their family *and* their souls.

It's all about putting yourself out there and getting the hands-on experience, and most likely, you're going to become passionate about something that you do. Internships and classes and other hands-on experiences could lead you to something that sparks your interest—the important thing is that you discover what's out there.

I think people are looking for that "Aha!" moment when this lightbulb goes off. And it's funny, because I never had that—I don't think I ever had that feeling. But I'm very passionate about what I do. And if you have that spark (lucky you!), you need to do something with it—that's when you know you're headed in the right direction.

CHAPTER 7

THE POWER OF OTHER PEOPLE

Nobody succeeds alone. I couldn't have started Benefab®, let alone built it to what it is today, without the support and feedback of many, many people—partners, vendors, customers, and more.

I started Benefab® with two partners and ended up with just one. Besides being a partner, Ron has become a mentor and has lent an incredible amount of knowledge to which I could never repay. He's a wise businessman and has supplied me with opportunity. I've also run with those opportunities, which has kept the partnership alive and well.

But he wasn't the only one guiding my journey. Looking back, I now realize how important it is to build relationships and learn from everyone you meet.

The Power of Relationships

It's easy to feel alone when first starting a business, and easy to feel limited by conventional wisdom. Many entrepreneurs think that no one will lend them money but a bank—and many times, the bank wants everything *plus* your right arm. This belief is not always the truth. There are good people out there with that hungry, excited enthusiasm that you have. There are private investors and venture capitalists that are willing to invest in *you*. There are people who will hurt you, but there are also people who will enrich you. If you are persistent and know what you want, you can and will achieve it. As mentioned before, I do believe in the law of attraction—if you know what you want, and you look for it, it many times, will present itself.

Still, when I started the business, there was a lot I didn't know. Googling was helpful. I did a lot of Googling! I also read a lot of books, and to be honest, I got caught up in the reading. The books seemed to complicate things, and I wasn't super-successful at reading "how-to" books. So, I joined an entrepreneurial circle, like a marketing insiders' club. Going to seminars and listening to presentations from successful people *who were already doing what I wanted to do* was very helpful. **I would say that the way I learned the most was by surrounding myself with people who were already doing what I wanted to do.** And that was a huge part of it: Putting myself in circles of people who I wanted to be like—other business owners and like-minded people in mastermind groups. I've noticed that changed me significantly. Even my outlook on life and materialistic things has changed; it's changed from being around the right people.

I've always been taught that the kind of people you spend time with is an indication of who you are. American entrepreneur, author, and motivational speaker Jim Rohn said, "You are the average of the five people you spend most of your time with." And I wholeheartedly believe that. Surrounding yourself with people you want to be like and who are where you want to be is so important. I frequently find myself sitting in a room with people who are far ahead of me in their entrepreneurial journeys, and that's just where I want to be. It's amazing—once you open yourself up to that, those people gravitate to you. People recognize hard work, and I've been blessed to meet people who've recognized that in me. They want to help people who are seizing opportunities and taking risks. Most entrepreneurs out there are self-made. They didn't get there without help from others, so most of the time, they can appreciate your struggle and are willing to offer you advice.

The biggest thing is, if you spend time with people who are scraping by, living paycheck to paycheck, that's your normal. If you're spending time with people who are flying in private jets and talking in thousands not hundreds, that becomes your normal. It becomes more and more familiar to you—more comfortable. Surround yourself with people whose normal is what you want your normal to be.

I experienced this for myself at an early age, even though I didn't consciously realize it at the time. Being in high school with kids from affluent families made me want that to be my normal, too.

I started going to that school as a sophomore in high school, so I had three years there, and those years really broadened my horizons enormously and steered me to what I really wanted out of life. So even then, my horizons were expanded by associating with people who had what I wanted to have and were doing what I wanted to be doing.

At that time, I had no idea of the path to get there, but I knew that I wanted more expendable income and a bigger life. Everyone has a different idea of success. To me it's emotional gratification and financial freedom.

Over the years, I've found that networking has made the world a lot more accessible; it has changed my whole outlook on business in its entirety—mine and others. Others have taught me that goals may continue to change. When you initially go into business, maybe your sales goal is $50,000 in the first year or even less. Then you reach $50,000—and no entrepreneur is going to stop at that destination. You're going to raise the bar, and your next goal will be $100,000, and when you reach that, your goal becomes a quarter of a million, so on and so forth.

For example, when I first started this journey, I believed I only wanted to sell exclusively to the show jumping world—because that was my normal. It was what was familiar to me: my comfort zone. **We are wired to stop taking action when something is out of our comfort zone; that is what stops us from taking risks and changing ourselves. I have learned to live outside that zone.**

Other business owners helped me recognize that I could expand outside of what I knew, which was a real eye-opener for me. I think a lot of people get married to the idea that "this is my niche." That's great if you want a very small business—stick to the one niche that you know and do it well, but realize that there is opportunity outside of that. It's a risk to seize it, but perhaps the reward will outweigh the risk. There's only one way to find out.

As you grow and begin to expand your grip on different audiences, you can multiply yourself by hiring more people, using intelligent software programs and implementing automation—with technology, you can do a lot. **Automation beats determination.** It has made goals reachable more quickly. I'm still far from where I envision myself in 10 years, but it's now more attainable than ever, because you see other people living it, and you think, "It's their world, so why can't it be mine?"

One thing I wish I'd known starting out was the importance of building relationships, since relationships with other successful people are the most important part of the journey. This should be about building real relationships with others, not just meeting them, shaking hands, and exchanging business cards. If they (or what they do) is of interest to you, take them to dinner and learn about them and have them learn about you. Most people want you to take an interest in them—that makes them feel appreciated (as they are). Then, they're willing to give you pointers and tips. Also, having the ability to pick up the phone and talk to somebody who's been there, done that is priceless.

If a relationship ends for whatever reason, I don't like leaving it behind with a bad taste in my mouth. There's always something good that somebody can give you. And at the end of every conversation, I try to take away one nugget and be able to put that in my toolbox. No one person can give you all the answers, but if they can give you one helpful tip, it may be a useful thing.

Also, in any relationship, you have to be able to take constructive criticism. A lot of people want to tell you everything you're doing wrong, and that's okay. You should listen because most of the time, they'll just talk themselves into telling you what you could do better. That being said, take it for what it's worth: Sometimes, it may be worth something. Other times, nothing. The only thing I can recommend is never take advice from someone who makes less money than you.

When I started, it was helpful that people would be honest enough with me to tell me when I was doing something wrong—like that my initial marketing efforts were too cluttered, and customers weren't going to waste ten minutes reading a magazine ad. And now with my public speaking, a lot of times professional speakers who hear me speak at a conference will come and say, "Hey, your speech was really great. I loved your presentation, but here's something that could make it a little better…"

A lot of people get defensive about constructive criticism and will counter the argument. Just stay quiet, you may learn something new.

This doesn't mean hanging your hat on every word those people say, but if they're successful people, they've got to know something, and they must be doing something right. Perhaps it's worth a listen.

And this holds for any industry. For example, I'm close to my banker, which is unusual today, but I think it's something useful. I talk to other people who exclusively use the ATM and mobile deposit. Personally, I like having a relationship—because if you need their help and you already know them personally, that does get you a long way. Now, when I walk into the bank, everyone knows me. How far will that get me? I have no idea. But I do know that it's much better to ask a favor of someone you know than it is to ask a stranger.

Looking back, what I should have done better five years ago was to take better advantage of those opportunities to get to know people I worked with. I've really started doing that in the past two years, much more so than I have in the past. To me, it's about learning someone's character, and if someone has a good character, I feel safe doing business with them. Developing trust and sharing the relationship outside of business can be very beneficial in business. This doesn't mean you necessarily have to become best friends, but if you're at a trade show or an event, invite them out to dinner and surround yourself with people you find interesting or want to be like—associating with other successful people changes the whole game.

Relationships are often mishandled in business: They either take up too much time and hold you back, or they aren't there at all. You can think of relationship building as networking on a scalable level. It can be tricky—networking can be kind of two-faced because focusing on your own local area can be distracting and take up an enormous amount of time, and it's not scalable. People can get tied down to local clubs and local organizations, and if you have a nationwide business, that's not going to help you. You must keep moving forward keeping your big picture goal in mind and remember it's the people you meet along the way that you should network with. But again, this depends on the business you're in—if you have a local shop, then it's great to do local networking.

And maybe your most important relationships are not just with potential clients, but people who've done well in their industry and can share their expertise. For instance, I've been talking to somebody who has sold to a big-box pet retailer in the past, and I'm trying to build that relationship, since I'm considering expanding our product line into the canine and feline markets. It's not that this person is going to get my products on the shelf at that store—I have no idea about that—but if we build our relationship, establish a trusting foundation,

Kat L. Chrysostom

who knows where it can lead? It comes down to surrounding yourself with people who are already where you want to be.

For me, this has mostly been people in retail—product-based businesses. I'm in such a niche market that I'm not in direct competition with them, so people are very willing to talk to me. I think they feel much less vulnerable; therefore, are willing to share more.

And it's one thing to surround yourself at a round table, but it's another to go to dinner with them and take interest in what they do. So, next time you pick up the phone to call, they know who you are—you aren't just a person on the other line. I think that level of trust goes a longer way than anything.

Building a Team

"Outstanding leaders go out of their way to boost the self-esteem of their personnel. If people believe in themselves, it's amazing what they can accomplish."
-Sam Walton

When I first started, I didn't have employees yet; I just hired a few independent contractors here and there. I think my control got in the way a little bit. At first, I was too demanding in some of the processes where people didn't need to be micromanaged, especially in tasks that required creativity. It took me a while to figure out that if you *manage and lead* people efficiently, they'll want to do things without you barking orders at them. That was probably the biggest learning curve, and looking back, I'm glad I went through that before I had employees.

But once Benefab® started to grow, I realized I needed a team to help me. I only have a small team, but each member is an integral part. I've been able to scale very well without having a large number of people because I have software systems in place to do what other employees would sometimes do.

Finding the right people can be a struggle. I ended up reaching out to my community through the local community college career board and they were very, very helpful. I found a couple of people, and one of the first people I hired is still with me—and I hope to have her for a long time. I knew what I wanted: someone who was young, that I could teach, who would do a bit of everything—and I found just what I was looking for.

In the beginning stages of starting a team, many times, you aren't able to hire for one thing (i.e. warehouse work, accounting, or answering phones, etc.). There simply isn't enough work in one department to afford one person for only that task. For me, that was the situation. I found someone with impeccable character who was enthusiastic, capable, and hungry. Those four things translated into a great employee who *wanted* to work for me. That one person is going to be crucial to scaling yourself. Once you find them, appreciate them. And you will perhaps begin to find your business growing beyond what you and your assistant can handle. Then you can begin hiring to delegate certain tasks.

How Do You Hire the Right People?

For us, age was an issue because we do a lot digitally, and social media marketing is a big part of the business. But I think that even more than that, it goes back to grit. Asking interview questions that measure their motivation is huge. I did not want to hire somebody who runs out of their list of things to do and sits around. Most importantly, what I've learned through this whole process is to hire people more for their personality, character traits, and morale than for what they know, because you can teach them what they need to know.

When I do interviews, I like to ask questions that show a person's imagination and motivation, such as where someone wants to be in five years or what they envision for retirement. Or who they're biggest role model is, or their favorite historical figure. To me those questions spark creativity. The answers to those questions can tell you a lot about someone such as what scale they think on (big vs. small), they're comfort with the world, and what they value most in someone (likely themselves, too).

Also, more than anything, I want to know if they have used and understand the products we sell. That's a big thing for me—are they believers in what we're doing? And obviously, that all fits into the brand mission. When you are interviewing someone, you should ask yourself, "Can I envision this person representing my company?" If you are being interviewed, you should ask yourself, "Can I envision myself representing this person and their company?"

I also interview to find out what trait is most important to a person. For me, it's character, because you can see how honest people are and how transparent they can be. You can see this in how they identify their own strengths and weaknesses—I think that's important because you learn how confident they are and if they're vulnerable enough to admit their weaknesses.

There are also tests and written evaluations that measure people skills and assess their strengths. One that is well-known is called the Wonderlic test, which some of my associates use in their hiring process. I would highly recommend using your own judgment in conjunction with any test, however.

Finally, one of my last questions, if I feel they're a strong candidate, is "What kind of boss do you work best for?" This question doesn't affect the decision to hire, but it affects the way I choose to lead. A lot of people want their employees to fit into one model of management. Maybe I'm sensitive to this because I grew up in the horse industry: Not every horse fits into one training model. With some horses, you have to change your training model to fit them better. It's the same thing with people—different people do best under different leadership, each person does best under a different structure.

I think having good leadership can make a good employee a great one; without leadership, they don't have any direction. You need a certain set of ingredients to be a good worker and a good employee, but I think it's primarily the leader's duty to give that employee the encouragement, direction, and tools to be the best they can be.

For me, that means understanding how everyone on my team is different and responds best to different kinds of leadership. I have a range of ages in the office, and each has their own way of working. It just depends on who it is. You learn to read people, and you learn to communicate in a way they understand— how do they feel most appreciated? It just depends on who the employee is. Daily, I work with about five people, and each of them has a different core—they require a different leadership style, and I can adapt to that, making them all feel appreciated, versus having an iron fist where they don't feel appreciated and don't *want* to work.

I think this approach is scalable if you begin to delegate that same structure into departments, but it requires a capable and empathetic leader in each department. For example, if you have a marketing department, a sales department, a research and development department, and an accounting department, each should have a competent leader. If you cannot communicate, you can't be a good leader. And, an employee should always have a leader to report back to—a lot of people in large corporate jobs get lost because they don't have anybody to report back to directly, and that ability is so important to one's success.

I learned this from being an employee before being a business owner—my bosses didn't communicate in the way that I did, and the entire organization lacked transparency. That experience really made me want to communicate at the level that my team members best understood and worked with.

I think this is important because in small business and leadership, perception becomes reality. If employees are seeing that you're a good leader and growing the business, then that becomes their reality in a sense. It's important to always maintain your enthusiasm in front of your employees, to keep them excited about the products, even if the business may be struggling behind closed doors—because what they're perceiving is what they're going to be showing to the end consumer.

My number one priority as a leader is that my employees feel appreciated, whether it's giving them a hug or telling them thank you. They do a lot, so I want them to know I'm grateful for that. Also, listening to their ideas, even if they are not great ideas, shows them that I appreciate their creativity. And if the idea is good, we can make it great by refining it to be something usable. But by far, it's important to make them feel appreciated, because if people feel appreciated, they want to work for you, and that serves everyone well.

Another thing I've learned is to let go and give them the freedom to develop their own ideas for the business. I see a lot of business owners who are far too controlling and don't give anyone leverage to be creative. I think you must be controlling in some sense because you have to keep your mission and your branding clear, but I think that if you rule the company with an iron fist, it shuts down creativity. Everything still goes through me before it goes out to the consumer, so the worst that can happen is someone comes up with something and I say "no, I don't like it." But if you give them that freedom—sometimes my employees come up with things I never, ever would have thought of, so it can really work in your favor if you let people be use their own mind.

Yes, it was a bit hard letting go of control at first. But I think being immersed in my bigger goals makes me focus on what I'm doing, so it's easier to give them a little more freedom. The farther away I got, the more leeway I give. **To grow, you must delegate.**

The more mistakes you make the better you become, so one way of getting over this was accepting that everything wasn't going to be perfect—when I make mistakes, I hold myself accountable for them, so when they make mistakes, I hold them accountable too. People want to be part of a team that's doing good things if they're well paid and appreciated—those two things play important roles.

Our company culture evolved pretty much organically, and I think in small businesses, that's the way it should be. My dad employed about 36 people before his practice was sold to a Fortune 500 company. But every morning, they had a morning huddle, they'd all pray together and set goals for the day. He always kept a small business atmosphere.

Where many small businesses get into trouble is when they start implementing bureaucratic policies—I see it happen all the time. When you're small, you should take advantage of the fact that you can do things one-on-one, and you really should capitalize on it. I've seen people implement complex policies with a staff of twenty. And I also watched my dad treat an office of 36 like it was family. No matter the structure, the ultimate desire should be one team working towards one goal.

I think it just depends on what you were exposed to and what you're most comfortable with. If you're transitioning from a corporate job to a career in small business, perhaps less policy will make you uncomfortable. Or vice versa. It depends on your business. There's no right or wrong answer, but for me, I like the more personal, one-on-one, family feeling. A wonderful example of a large company that has successfully scaled this "family" feel is Chewy.com—if you're a customer of theirs, you likely understand what I mean by this. In the process of growing their customer base to 3 million+, they have solely focused their efforts on efficiency and customer service—employing people to answer phones and texts around the clock. According to an article published in Forbes, the founder of Chewy.com, Ryan Cohen, "sleeps three hours a night, reading feedback on Chewy's Facebook page into the wee hours. Positive reviews, he says, 'give me goose bumps.'"

I also work with a handful of independent contractors at any given time: IT, technical design, some creative development, and graphic design. When selecting an outside contractor, I feel it's very important that they learn the business and they know what we're about—similar to an in-house employee, but not as in depth, of course.

For overall team management, my biggest stressor is transparency and making sure each member knows what the goals are in the business. For my team, this makes them feel like a bigger part of the picture—and most importantly, they begin to envision that goal, also.

The Most Important People in Your Business: Your Customers

Another hard lesson I learned was that building relationships with customers is essential.

The first step in the conversation is connecting with people. People love to hear their names, so if they're wearing any kind of name badge, calling them by name is an excellent way to open a conversation. But instead of going straight into the sale, learn what they are looking for and see if you can help in potentially solving their problem. Always remember, a good sales conversation is not about you; it should be about the potential customer/client. If you're in a retail store or at a trade show and the client is present, remember that sometimes people don't want to be talked to, and you can tell (they're looking at the ground, if their shoulders are slightly slouched forward, or their arms are crossed). Many times, body language can tell you more about a person faster than them speaking.

Learning to accurately read body language and faces is a big part of communication, because that's the first thing that registers. I read a book about reading people in the first seven seconds of meeting them, and it helped me, but more than anything, the act of doing it over and over taught me best.

I've talked to hundreds, if not thousands, of people about my products, and with each conversation, my communication becomes better and better. But there's a psychological role in selling—I think to be a good entrepreneur, you must be a good marketer, therefore you have to sell. And to really sell well, you should understand psychology. I'd recommend that any entrepreneur read up on psychology and get to know the way we think, such as how we make buying decisions—one side of the brain drives emotions and is often what is used at the point of purchase. The other side is the logical side, which normally helps someone explain their purchase decision. Good salesmanship is an art involving body language, communication, and psychology—each of those things greatly influence the sales process.

I also read a great book on body language that I purchased before traveling overseas. It was about different cultures and body language within those cultures which has been helpful for me in my travels abroad.

Also, once somebody begins to talk, you can tell what kind of engagement they want. Within the first few seconds, you'll know, okay, he's more technical, or she's more of an emotional person, etc.—this information will steer the conversation to talking about the features of a product/service versus only the benefits. You will learn what to talk about to who. And that knowledge will customize the conversation.

For the first two years, I was kind of stumbling through, because I, like a lot of other people, underestimated the value of personalized sales—especially as an entrepreneur. Many entrepreneurs aren't necessarily in sales, but they're forced to sell. They may be great inventors and may have originated an awesome idea, but they don't know how to sell it. So, you have to shake that—some people are naturally good salesmen, but understanding how the mind works and body language can make you a great one.

Above all, it's important to never forget your customers are people— they have wants and fears and good days and bad days, just like the rest of us. Remembering this whenever I engage them has not only been good for sales, it feels right too—because remembering that we're helping real people and seeing how our products improve lives is the best part of my business.

Expert Tip: The Power of Listening

As Kat has covered, there are many different factors that go into truly communicating with your clients/customers. Body language is visibly obvious, but what about the not so obvious? What I am talking about is all the stories, past and beliefs the person you are talking to has within their mind and heart. Communication is more than body poses, words, and tones. Truly it is an art form to engage with people on an authentic level.

I grew up in a home where I didn't feel I had a voice. No didn't mean no. I spent a lifetime swallowing my words which ultimately almost cost me my life. As a result of my past experiences, I am committed to making sure that every one person can find their voice. I created a communication tool that helps people identify whom they are speaking with whether it is an email, on the phone or in person by identify their personality language. I have the privilege of traveling across the globe teaching this system to organizations, boards, entrepreneurs and individuals like you. But what do you do if you haven't been trained in a personality language system? You listen!

In my "Compassionate Courageous Conversations" keynote I teach how to move past the uncomfortable and engage in true authentic conversation. I encourage people to listen and I am not talking about listening to respond. I am talking about listening to H.E.A.R.

H—to listen with your Heart free of distractions, judgment, or blame. Most people want to share their true feelings, yet they do not because they fear what we would think of them if we knew their truth. When we put our stories, past and experiences on hold for a brief moment, we create a safe place for others to truly connect with us.

E—to have Empathy and to be fully present in the moment. This is the biggest gift we can give to another human being to just hear them. Think about it, how often do you find yourself wishing someone would just hear you?

A—to Accept them where they are in that moment. That doesn't mean you have to agree with them, just understand where they are coming from. For them their beliefs are very real, based on their experiences, just as yours are and why you feel different. It is OK for us to be different.

R—to Relate is to find a common ground. It does not mean we need to one up their story. When we share our stories, it can appear as a competition of scars. Most cases we are just innocently trying to show we can relate, but it could make them feel like you listened to respond.

I often say, "we are one conversation away from compassion" because we are if we are willing to HEAR. When we can come to every conversation whether with our clients, customers or personally to truly HEAR, we transform our relationships. Think about it. People do business with people they like. If you give the gift of truly hearing someone, that is priceless. Who wouldn't want to do business or refer business to someone who truly "gets" them?

Happy Connecting,

Claudia Jean Virga
Professional Speaker & Author
www.ClaudiaJeanSpeaker.com

CHAPTER 8

MOVING FORWARD

Benefab® has grown and changed in many ways since the beginning. When I first started, I'd get maybe two or three emails a day about the company. And every time we got an order, I'd have to drop everything and run down to our storage unit (at the time) to ship it.

Now, I receive between 60-70 emails a day and I do a lot more work, but it just feels natural to me—it all part of the process.

We started in a 10'x10' storage unit. And as the company grew, I moved into an airport T-hangar, because it was the most affordable space. Now we have a warehouse with a small, but formal office space with workstations.

It's a good place to work, and I feel that I can be a good leader to the employees and encourage them, since I know exactly what they're doing and what they're going through because I've done every aspect of this business myself. The idea of a CEO coming into a company without ever having worked on the ground floor is nonsense in my opinion. Even if you don't stay in a position for a long time, you should still know the ropes starting at the ground level.

My days are busy, but much more organized than they used to be. Things that I used to handle alone have been delegated, and although I'm just as involved as I used to be, my position has morphed into more of a managerial, leadership role, which allows me much more time to focus on growth of the company overall.

Now, when we go to trade shows, we're no longer blindsided by other set-ups and vendors—we're completely prepared (almost) every time and continue to set much higher expectations for ourselves in terms of ROI.

For the first few years, if we could break even, we'd look at it as a marketing experience. For us, the challenge is we have a technical sale—our products are not an impulse buy. So, selling our products may be a very different experience than that of entrepreneurs who do offer impulse products.

For the first year and a half, our efforts were about educating the market-place—a long and challenging process. At the break-even point, I considered it an investment in time and sweat equity. And this ended up really paying off for us—we went to every venue we could afford, and if we could make more money than we'd invested, we were happy. I just kept building on that by collecting contact information from interested people and following up. We've educated a lot of people that way.

We set a goal for every show, and we do a daily breakdown, which helps us break our goal into smaller, more attainable numbers. Now we're growing with every show that we do, and we're much more selective about the audiences that we choose. I like to see a twenty- to thirty- percent increase in sales at each trade show per year (meaning our second time at the same venue).

I map out our calendar for trade shows. Every fourth quarter, we start scheduling the next year's schedule, and we select the best ones from the previous year and see which ones we may want to add. If a trade show has dropped in foot traffic or sales, we take it off the list. If we can educate a lot of people, then it could be worth the investment—those decisions are made on an individual basis.

Another thing I'm always doing to move the business ahead is reading business magazines and books to keep myself educated on what's working well for other businesses. The equine industry, as I've mentioned, tends to be a bit old-fashioned, so I've learned to apply a lot of strategies other industries are using successfully.

For instance, one of my favorite magazines had an article about how a lot of jobs are being lost to robots, and how artificial intelligence is replacing many jobs. This article was specifically talking about women in the workplace. And one thing that artificial intelligence can't replace is empathy. This relates back to the possible advantages that people (particularly women) in business may have.

And this felt so true, even though it doesn't relate directly to the equine market: What people are really looking for is empathy. So, I like to read those tidbits, take that knowledge, and apply it to my business. That is something that we offer—this unique customer experience customized to that one person, so they feel that we empathize with their situation. Knowledge like this should spur questions: How can we be more empathetic? How can we cater more to our customers? And how can we use readily available resources to deliver our empathy?

Our focus on empathy has had another great benefit too—even though we have a significant online presence, we rarely ever receive a bad online review. I think this is because for the most part, we don't really capitalize on people who are not our ideal customer. I always tell my employees who work sales—"we're not selling products, we're providing solutions." I think most of the time, if someone is your ideal customer, if the product doesn't work out, they'll just contact us to do an exchange or a refund. I've had few and far between complaints, but most of the time that's when I will step in—thankfully, this is a rare occasion. I'll call the customer directly and see if there's any way to salvage the situation, and if there isn't, we offer a refund, so everybody's happy. The customer then goes away feeling like they were taken care of to the best of our ability. This is why taking the time to address those customers is essential.

With our plans for expansion into the feline and canine markets, we'll have to start relating to a whole new group of customers with completely different expectations, so our marketing and ways of relating to customers will have to evolve. I think that the canine and feline market is more pet-oriented, so it's more emotional—you don't sleep with your horse. People think of their horses as pets and they love them, but it's a different emotional connection than a person has with their dog or cat. Our marketing will reflect these differences, which will be a lot of fun.

For me, continuing to learn is key.

I don't trust a lot of so-called business gurus. Listening to a lot of how-to books on how to start a business can be confusing. Many times, it's bad advice because you can't tell people how to run a business—you can only say, "this worked for me—try it in your industry."

The most important thing about running a business is persistence and implementation. I see a lot of people saying, "Well, I built a multi-million-dollar business, and you could do this too, if you just listen to me."

Not so!

If that was the case, everyone would be doing it. The best way to do anything is to just take action and do it. Prepare as much as you can, but most importantly, just get out there and start. You'll learn a lot along the way and be able to perfect it as you go. Just listening to advice that worked for someone else isn't enough—you must take the leap.

EPILOGUE

L ooking back, I guess it's no surprise that my relationship with horses has been such a huge part of who I am and how I learned about the world.

My mom rode horses when she was a child and has always loved them, as did my dad when he was a little boy. But my father's brother, my Uncle Lex, had gotten killed on a horse when he was only nine years old.

It was a neighbor friend's pony, and it was wearing a halter and a lead rope, but no bit, bridle, or saddle. Lex was young and had gotten on the pony after the neighbors asked if he wanted a pony ride back to the barn. When they let go, the pony took off toward the barn. But the lead rope was tied, and poor Lex got his leg caught in it and was dragged for an extended period of time. He was basically stuck underneath the pony. He was on life support with slim chances of survival. That was a long time ago, too, so the medicine wasn't nearly as good as it is today.

As expected, this was horribly traumatic for my Yia-Yia and Pappou. It seemed that my grandfather kind of got past it; my grandmother never let that go.

And that was a serious part of my childhood because it was very difficult for my paternal grandparents to accept that my dad would ever allow horses into our household. So, I've always known there was a risk to riding and was as cautious as one could be.

That was a huge reason why we didn't have horses from the get-go. My mom begged and begged to have a horse. Then one day, a woman came into my father's dental office needing a full smile restoration but couldn't afford it. She ended up trading her beautiful Arabian dressage horse for a beautiful smile. This was how my mom eventually convinced my dad to get a horse.

That was when I was two years old, and my first ride was the day that horse arrived. At the farm, my mom and I saddled up and went double-riding. We stayed out for hours—she could not wait for anyone to come and watch me! We still laugh about that.

And I never stopped riding—I was always passionate about horses. My first formal lesson was on my fourth birthday. That was with my trainer, Rose Marie, whose only rule was you couldn't start lessons until you were five—but my love of horses was stronger than her willpower. I trained with her for ten years. She taught me to ride and was really an integral part of my early life. And since then, I have not let go.

Until the accident.

They say that when you fall off a horse, the best thing to do is get right back on again, before you get the chance to get spooked by the experience. That clearly wasn't an option for me. But I knew I had to get back to riding again—I wanted to do it because I didn't want to let the past define my future, and because I never lost the passion for it.

But getting back into riding was harder than I thought. Several months after I got out of the hospital, I tried to ride again. I honestly thought I wouldn't have a problem with it—I thought I'd get onto the horse and everything would be like before.

But it wasn't—getting up the nerve to ride again was much harder than I ever imagined.

When I did try to ride again, I had a small pony—well, technically, he was a large pony, but he was very small compared to what I was used to riding. His name was Edelweiss, and he had the kindest soul—he rebuilt my confidence. I did a tiny bit every day with him. I walked with him for months, then I started to do a little bit more, and incrementally, I became more and more comfortable.

Graduating to horses was more difficult. But I knew that to better myself and to keep getting back into riding, I'd have to part ways with Edelweiss. Then I got a horse, and I think that's what made me realize I was never going to get back to where I'd been—it's when I realized that I would never have that confidence or the aspirations I had as a rider before the accident.

That's when I started shifting my focus and focusing more on young horses and doing more groundwork than work in the saddle. I've found a niche within the riding industry where I am comfortable and confident. Young horses improve so quickly, and it's been a rewarding and fun change. I've sort of reinvented myself to do something that's completely different from what I was doing before, but it's still with horses and I'm able to have an outlet for that passion, but the end goal has changed. So, I still ride, but I don't jump. I still work with show horses as a hobby, but I have them when they're young—I walk, trot, and canter with them, and I teach them the basics. I'm just coming in much earlier in their training—I used to be at the finishing end, now I'm at the beginning.

In the talks that I do, I talk about these experiences—these changes. I talk about the accident, then my shift from Quest to Benefab®. Then I talk about the things I did in those situations—and one of these things is instead of accepting the defeat, I reinvented what I was doing, and instead of ever saying "I can't," I said, "I will."

This wasn't an easy transition. And I think before having any kind of accident, you think you are invincible, which is such a blessing—because when you don't have that fear, you can truly live life to the fullest. I feel like I did do that before I had my accident. And I still live life to the fullest, but in a different light.

It was very scary to get back on, but just the idea of doing it—doing it over and over again until I started to become comfortable—kept me going.

Thinking back on all this reminds me something a business mentor once told me, when someone else was throwing around the old expression "failure is not an option": He reminded me that failure *is* a possibility—but it's what you choose to do when you fail that makes or breaks you.

You have to get back on that horse again. It may take weeks or months to do it, it may be hard, and it may not be anything like you thought it would be—it certainly wasn't for me. But in the end, the ride is so worth it.

ACKNOWLEDGEMENTS

Without the help of many, many people, this book would not have come to fruition. Not just the writing part, but everything in between the lines. For those many people who have supported me along this journey and believed in me from the start, I thank you from the bottom of my heart.

To each successful and tumultuous situation, I have learned equally as much and am thankful for the experience.

I thank my family, friends, business associates, and partners for their support. Especially to my parents, Mom and Dad, for instilling in me a nurturing spirit combined with a fiery passion for success. And to my brother and sisters, who are always there when I need them.

To my horses and animals, I thank you for the company and relationships that I have been able to share with each of you—for helping me keep my sanity in the busiest of times and the unconditional love that you show me every day. And to God—for his infinite love and forgiveness that never ceases to amaze me.

I also thank my editor and advisor, Felicia Lee—without you and your talent, this book would never have been possible. And lastly, to Richard—for the opportunity to a bigger, better life.

Notes

8. *40.2 percent of the Fortune 500 firms in 2016 were founded by immigrants and/ or their children:* New American Economy (2016) "Reason for Reform: Entrepreneurship" October, http://www.newamericaneconomy.org/wp-content/uploads/2016/12/Entrepreneur.pdf

13. *Free, US based URL search engine:* https://www.godaddy.com/

13. *Free, filed trademark search engine:* https://www.trademarkia.com/

13. *Free, granted patent search engine:* https://www.google.com/patents

14. *80% of entrepreneurs who start their own business fail within the first 18 months:* Wagner, Eric T., Forbes, (2013) "Five Reasons 8 out 10 Businesses Fail" September 12, https://www.forbes.com/sites/ericwagner/2013/09/12/five-reasons-8-out-of-10-businesses-fail/#55a049066978

16. *Your Body Language May Shape Who Your Are:* Cuddy, Amy, TED talk, June 2012. https://www.ted.com/talks/amy_cuddy_your_body_language_shapes_who_you_are

26. *people spend on average 10 hours per day using some sort of screen:* Howard, Jacqueline, CNN (2016) "Americans devote more than 10 hours a day to screen time, and growing" July 29, https://www.cnn.com/2016/06/30/health/americans-screen-time-nielsen/index.html

40. *Disney debuted his first full-length film,* **Snow White and the Seven Dwarfs***, which, because of the Great Depression, was not expected to do well:* Lamble, Ryan. (2014) "Disney's Snow White: the risk that changed filmmaking forever" November 25, http://www.denofgeek.com/us/movies/snow-white/241629/disneys-snow-white-the-risk-that-changed-filmmaking-forever

40. *[James Dyson] worked 5 years and had 5,127 prototypes before succeeding in the creation of a bag-less vacuum:* Malone-Kircher, Madison (2016) "James Dyson on 5,126 Vacuums That Didn't Work — and the One That Finally Did" November 22, http://nymag.com/vindicated/2016/11/james-dyson-on-5-126-vacuums-that-didnt-work-and-1-that-did.html

71. *The Wonderlic Test:* https://www.wonderlic.com/

74. *family feel at chewy.com:* Adams, Susan, Forbes (2017) "The Man Who Found Gold in Dog Food" January 24, https://www.forbes.com/sites/susan-adams/2017/01/10/the-man-who-found-gold-in-dog-food/#f44e09830957

86. *Editor and Advisor:* https://www.felicialeewrites.com/

Made in the USA
Columbia, SC
20 March 2018